# From Operator to Entrepreneur

Leveraging Vision, Technology,
and Leadership to Drive Business Success

Maria L. Ellis, MBA

Washington, DC, USA

Copyright © Maria L. Ellis, 2024

All rights reserved. No part of this book may be reproduced in any form without permission in writing from the author. Reviewers may quote brief passages in reviews.

Published 2024

DISCLAIMER

No part of this publication may be reproduced or transmitted in any form or by any means, mechanical or electronic, including photocopying or recording, or by any information storage and retrieval system, or transmitted by email without permission in writing from the author.

Neither the author nor the publisher assumes any responsibility for errors, omissions, or contrary interpretations of the subject matter herein. Any perceived slight of any individual or organization is purely unintentional.

Brand and product names are trademarks or registered trademarks of their respective owners.

# DEDICATION

To the dedicated entrepreneurs and business operators who strive for excellence beyond the ordinary. This book is for those who aim to make their businesses thrive, not just survive, and who are ready to embrace change, lead with vision, and achieve new levels of growth.

To my beloved husband, Stephen William Ellis, founder of Newstex, LLC, our news and media aggregator, whose passion and vision continue to inspire me every day.

To my incredible team, whose commitment makes every goal possible, and to my loving family, for your unwavering support and belief in my journey.

And to all the leaders who seek to rise above the daily grind, becoming the visionary architects of their own success – may this book be a guide on your path.

## ADVANCE PRAISE

"Maria L. Ellis has crafted an essential guide for business leaders seeking entrepreneurial success. From Operator to Entrepreneur: Leveraging Vision, Technology, and Leadership to Drive Business Success is a treasure trove of knowledge, blending innovative strategies with proven techniques and actionable insights. With real-world examples and practical advice, Maria provides a clear roadmap that will inspire entrepreneurs to achieve sustainable growth and lasting success. Well done, Maria!"
— Geoff Taylor, President & CEO, c3controls & c3digitus; Founding Member, Evolute Pickleball, Tally Scoreboards, and 2EC, USA

"Artificial intelligence is often seen as a tool reserved for large corporations, but Maria L. Ellis, MBA skillfully dispels this myth. In From Operator to Entrepreneur: Leveraging Vision, Technology, and Leadership to Drive Business Success she demonstrates how even small and medium-sized businesses can leverage AI to unlock new opportunities. Maria's deep experience in nurturing entrepreneurs' shines through as she guides readers on how to harness this technology effectively. Her insights on customizing AI applications for practical, everyday use are invaluable. This book is a must-read for anyone looking to transform their business and capitalize on the emerging 'tree of knowledge' in today's digital age."
— Antonio Segna, Business Owner, Italy

"From Operator to Entrepreneur: Leveraging Vision, Technology, and Leadership to Drive Business Success is an essential read for any business owner looking to elevate their company. Maria L. Ellis challenges leaders to lift their heads from the daily grind, adopt a broader perspective, and embrace innovation as a driving force.

Drawing from real-world case studies, Ellis demonstrates how clinging to micro-management or resisting change can cause businesses to miss valuable opportunities. This book offers a practical, hands-on guide to overcoming these pitfalls, featuring specific technology tools and platforms to help entrepreneurs evolve into visionary leaders.

Reading From Operator to Entrepreneur is an inspiring way to spark creativity and learn actionable strategies to propel your business into the future."

— Diane Drey, Founder, Money 101 Education, New York A Financial Literacy Program for Women, USA

"From Operator to Entrepreneur: Leveraging Vision, Technology, and Leadership to Drive Business Success is a must-read for any business owner looking to elevate their company beyond the daily grind. Maria L. Ellis offers a compelling roadmap for transforming from an operator to a visionary leader. This book is filled with actionable strategies that every entrepreneur can benefit from. "
— Joey Antonio, Chairman, Century Properties Group Inc., Philippines

"From Operator to Entrepreneur: Leveraging Vision, Technology, and Leadership to Drive Business Success is a brilliant synthesis of vision, leadership, and technology. Maria L. Ellis not only shows you what's possible but gives you the tools to make it happen. A truly invaluable resource for today's business owners. "

— Charles Rothschild, Chairman of the Board, Fiberstar, Inc., Brazil

"Maria L. Ellis has distilled decades of experience into a practical guide for business owners. Her insights on leadership, technology, and scaling up are transformative. This book, From Operator to Entrepreneur: Leveraging Vision, Technology, and Leadership to Drive Business Success, should be on the desk of every entrepreneur who wants to stay ahead of the curve."
— James Lee, Lee World Group founder, China

"If you're serious about taking your business to the next level, read this book, From Operator to Entrepreneur: Leveraging Vision, Technology, and Leadership to Drive Business Success Maria L. Ellis offers a clear and compelling strategy for stepping out of daily operations and embracing the role of a visionary leader. Her advice on leveraging AI alone is worth the read."
— Dr. C.S. Rani, Professor, CIS Department, BMCC, The City University of New York

# TABLE OF CONTENTS

| | |
|---|---|
| Foreword | i |
| Chapter 1: The Entrepreneur versus the Business Operator | 1 |
| Chapter 2: Understanding the Business You're In | 27 |
| Chapter 3: The Business You Should Be In | 39 |
| Chapter 4: Embracing New Technologies | 53 |
| Chapter 5: Harnessing AI for Business Growth | 71 |
| Chapter 6: Moving Beyond Operations | 89 |
| Chapter 7: Scaling for Success | 103 |
| Chapter 8: Future-Proofing Your Business | 123 |
| Chapter 9: The Entrepreneur's Journey | 141 |
| Chapter 10: A Final Wish for Your Entrepreneurial Journey | 151 |
| Chapter 11: Crafting a Visionary Business Culture | 161 |
| Chapter 12: Creating Impact Beyond Profit | 169 |
| Chapter 13: Nurturing the Entrepreneur Within (Bonus Chapter) | 175 |

# FOREWORD

If you're a small business owner feeling overwhelmed by the demands of daily operations, this book is your ticket to freedom. *From Operator to Entrepreneur: Leveraging Vision, Technology, and Leadership to Drive Business Success* isn't just another collection of business theories—it's a practical, no-nonsense guide to stepping up as a leader and transforming your business.

What sets this book apart is its focus on action. Maria L. Ellis doesn't just outline what you need to do—she shows you how to do it. From shifting your mindset as an operator to stepping into the role of a visionary leader, this book walks you through the process with clarity and purpose. Whether it's streamlining operations, adopting cutting-edge technology, or mastering leadership strategies that drive real results, this guide has everything you need to elevate your business.

Filled with actionable insights, powerful case studies, and a practical roadmap for harnessing AI and other transformative tools, this book is a catalyst for change. It's more than a guide to growing your business—it's a blueprint for securing its future. If you're ready to escape the daily grind, lead with clarity and vision, and realize your full potential as an entrepreneur, this is the resource you've been looking for.

— Jayant Davar, Chairman, Managing Director, and CEO, Sandhar, India

# CHAPTER 1:
# THE ENTREPRENEUR VERSUS THE BUSINESS OPERATOR

*"Imagination is everything. It is the preview of life's coming attractions."*
– Albert Einstein

As a business owner, I have often encountered countless peers who, despite their best intentions, have found themselves trapped in the role of an operator rather than thriving as true entrepreneurs. The distinction between these two roles is critical, yet it's often overlooked. An entrepreneur is a visionary, a leader who sees the big picture and strategically drives the business toward growth, innovation, and success. They are focused on long-term goals, constantly seeking new opportunities to expand their company, and leveraging resources to maximize potential.

On the other hand, an operator is someone who gets caught up in the day-to-day tasks and operations of the business. Instead of steering the ship toward new horizons, they're down in the engine room changing light bulbs – tasks any crew member could handle. Meanwhile, opportunities sail right past their business.

While operations are essential to the success of any business, when the owner becomes too involved in these tasks, they lose sight of the broader goals. The operator is focused on maintaining the status quo, ensuring that the daily processes run smoothly, but often at the expense of growth and innovation. The key difference lies in perspective: the entrepreneur works on the business, creating strategies for growth and innovation, while the operator works in the business, managing daily operations. Are you trapped working in your business instead of leading it? You're not alone. As a business owner, I have watched countless talented entrepreneurs get stuck in the weeds of daily operations. I am reminded of my friend Alex, an entrepreneur and founder of a medium-sized news and media aggregator, who prefers to be the business operator managing the daily operations of his company and troubleshooting any immediate challenges that arise instead of creating strategies for the company's future success. As the entrepreneur, Alex should focus on the company's growth and future. Alex should spend his time developing partnerships with new content providers, exploring the use of AI to deliver more personalized news feeds, and planning an expansion into international markets.

## The Million-Dollar Mindset Shift

The mindset of an entrepreneur is fundamentally different from that of an operator. Entrepreneurs are driven by creativity, innovation, and a desire to build something larger than themselves. They are constantly thinking about how to scale the business, enter new markets, and stay ahead of the competition. Their focus is on growth, and they are not afraid to take calculated risks to achieve it.

When faced with a market downturn, operators cut costs and hunker down. Entrepreneurs? They see the perfect moment to acquire struggling competitors or innovate new solutions while others retreat. This allows them to focus on the strategic aspects of the business, such as forging new partnerships, exploring new markets, and innovating products or services.

In contrast, operators tend to have a more conservative mindset. They are often more risk-averse, focusing on efficiency and maintaining the current state of the business. Their primary concern is keeping the business running smoothly, which often leads them to micromanage and take on tasks that could be delegated. This mindset can stifle growth because it limits the business to its current capabilities and prevents the exploration of new opportunities.

For business owners, adopting an entrepreneurial mindset is crucial. It's about shifting from being consumed by daily operations to thinking strategically about the future of the business. This shift in mindset is essential for driving growth and ensuring long-term success.

The following are some examples of how businesses have missed opportunities or failed to grow because the business owner became too focused on being an operator rather than a thriving entrepreneur:

### 1. *The Retailer Who Stagnated*

Taylor's Treasures was a mid-sized, family-owned retailer specializing in vintage and handmade home decor items. Located in several small cities, the store had a loyal local following and a unique collection that stood out from big-box retailers. However, as the world moved increasingly online, Taylor's Treasures stuck to its traditional in-store model. The owner, Taylor, was comfortable with the familiar operations of running physical stores and was reluctant to embrace e-commerce, believing customers would continue to visit in person for the store's unique, curated experience.

When online retail began booming, Taylor missed several major opportunities:

Online Marketplace Presence: Competitors in similar niches quickly joined platforms like Etsy, Amazon, and eBay. They reached a wider audience and capitalized on the growing trend of customers shopping for unique home decor online. Taylor's Treasures, however, chose not to explore these platforms, missing out on potential new customers.

Own E-commerce Site: Taylor delayed building an e-commerce site for years, thinking it was too costly and complex. When the store finally launched a basic site, it lacked an efficient checkout process, had limited payment options, and was hard to navigate on mobile devices. As a result, it struggled to convert visitors into buyers, and many frustrated customers left to shop with competitors.

Social Media and Digital Marketing: While competitors invested in targeted social media ads, influencer partnerships, and email marketing campaigns, Taylor's Treasures relied on word of mouth and occasional in-store promotions. This strategy failed to attract new demographics and grow beyond the local customer base.

Consequences: Within five years, Taylor's Treasures saw revenue drop by nearly 30 percent. The store's market share shrank as competitors gained a strong online presence, reaching not only local but also national and even international customers. The lack of an e-commerce strategy and digital presence left Taylor's Treasures outpaced, and the store became known as "outdated" and "hard to access" among younger customers. Eventually, Taylor was forced to close two of the four physical locations and lay off several employees, significantly scaling back the business.

This stagnation could have been avoided if Taylor had embraced e-commerce and digital marketing earlier. By remaining focused solely on in-store operations and overlooking the changing retail landscape, Taylor's Treasures was left behind, losing both revenue and relevance in the rapidly evolving market.

Missed Opportunity: Olivia's Organics, a family-owned specialty grocery store, had been a community staple for over two decades. Known for high-quality organic produce, gourmet ingredients, and unique local products, the store drew a loyal crowd of health-conscious locals. Despite its success, Olivia, the owner, remained skeptical about e-commerce. She believed customers preferred in-store shopping to experience the fresh produce and specialty items firsthand. Convinced that the personal touch of a physical store couldn't be replicated online, she chose not to invest in a website, online ordering, or delivery options.

Meanwhile, competitors in the organic grocery sector began adapting rapidly.

- E-Commerce Sites and Online Ordering: Competing stores and new online-only players invested heavily in user-friendly websites that offered a full selection of organic produce and gourmet items. Customers could browse, order, and schedule home deliveries or in-store pickups.
- Subscription Boxes: Many retailers launched subscription services that allowed customers to receive fresh, organic produce weekly or monthly. Olivia's Organics missed this opportunity, overlooking a growing trend in the grocery industry.
- Digital Advertising and Social Media: Competitors leveraged social media and digital marketing to showcase their offerings, post customer testimonials, and run promotions. Olivia's Organics, however, relied solely on word of mouth and occasional in-store flyers, missing the chance to reach new, tech-savvy customers in neighboring communities and beyond.

Consequences: Over time, Olivia's Organics began losing its market share. With more options for convenient online grocery shopping, even loyal customers started to favor competitors, especially during busy periods or harsh weather. Within a few years, Olivia's Organics saw a 40 percent drop in revenue. Additionally, competitors who expanded online gained visibility across the region, capturing the attention of health-conscious consumers willing to pay a premium for organic goods delivered to their doors.

By staying focused solely on brick-and-mortar, Olivia's Organics not only missed significant revenue opportunities but also lost relevance as online shopping became the norm in the grocery sector. Unable to pivot quickly to a digital model, Olivia eventually downsized the business, struggling to sustain the store in a marketplace dominated by e-commerce-savvy competitors.

## 2. *The Tech Startup That Lost Its Edge*

BrightTrack, a tech startup, launched with a revolutionary software product aimed at project management for small businesses. The software was fast, customizable, and tailored to meet the unique needs of small teams, and it quickly attracted a strong customer base. The founder, Sam, was not only the visionary behind BrightTrack but also its lead developer. As a technical expert with a passion for coding, Sam spent most of his time refining the core product and personally handling customer support tickets to ensure the platform worked flawlessly.

In its early days, this hands-on approach was effective. However, as the market evolved and competitors entered the space, BrightTrack started falling behind:

- Competitors' New Features: Rival companies began introducing features like AI-powered project insights, customizable dashboards, and integrations with popular third-party apps. Customers started asking for these improvements, but Sam was so absorbed in troubleshooting bugs and responding to support requests that he lacked the bandwidth to innovate. He was constantly "in the weeds" with the product, and these emerging needs went largely unaddressed.
- User Experience and Interface: While BrightTrack's backend was solid, competitors invested in intuitive, visually appealing interfaces that enhanced the user experience. BrightTrack's interface, however, remained basic and dated. Customers started to view the platform as functional but uninspiring, favoring more user-

friendly alternatives with modern design.
- Marketing and Strategic Growth: Sam's time and focus were so absorbed by coding and customer support that BrightTrack had no dedicated team for marketing, partnerships, or strategic planning. As competitors ramped up marketing efforts and expanded their reach, BrightTrack remained largely invisible outside of its initial customer base, missing opportunities to capture a wider audience.

Consequences: Over the next two years, BrightTrack's growth stalled. The company's market share declined as customers migrated to competitors offering advanced features and a more engaging user experience. Despite having a technically sound product, BrightTrack lost its edge because it failed to innovate and adapt to the market's evolving demands. Eventually, the company's revenue declined sharply, and Sam was forced to consider selling BrightTrack or merging with a competitor to stay afloat.

This example shows how focusing solely on operational tasks can hold back a startup's growth. By not stepping back to work on the business – investing in new features, user experience, and strategic marketing – Sam's startup was unable to keep pace with competitors and ultimately lost its position in the market.

### *3. The Restaurant That Didn't Scale*

Chef Marco's Bistro was a popular, family-owned restaurant that became a local favorite in its town. Known for its authentic Italian dishes made from scratch, along with a welcoming, personal atmosphere, Chef Marco's Bistro attracted a loyal following. Chef Marco, the owner and head chef, was deeply involved in every aspect of the restaurant – he personally created the daily menu, prepared many of the signature dishes, and often spent time mingling with customers to ensure everyone enjoyed their meal. His hands-on approach and attention to detail became part of the restaurant's charm, giving it a unique, intimate feel.

With rave reviews, regular customers, and growing recognition from food bloggers, Chef Marco's Bistro had the potential to expand:

- Opening New Locations: Many customers and food critics suggested that Marco open additional locations in nearby cities, where similar authentic Italian dining experiences were in demand. The bistro's brand and reputation made it well-positioned for regional expansion.
- Franchising Opportunities: Several investors approached Marco about franchising the brand. They envisioned Chef Marco's Bistro as a successful chain, introducing its distinctive Italian flavors and atmosphere to new audiences. However, franchising required documented recipes, standardized processes, and trained managers – steps Marco hadn't taken because he was so personally involved in every detail.

Challenges to Scaling: Marco's reluctance to step back from daily operations prevented him from pursuing these opportunities. Rather than building a team and documenting the restaurant's core processes, he remained "in the business," overseeing each meal and handling customer issues himself. He was hesitant to delegate, feeling that no one could replicate the level of care he brought to the bistro. Consequently, essential tasks for scaling – such as creating a scalable menu, training systems, and brand guidelines – were left unaddressed.

Consequences: Within a few years, competitors in nearby areas started offering similar Italian dining experiences. Chef Marco's Bistro continued to thrive locally, but it was effectively "capped" in terms of growth. New customers from outside the area had limited access to the bistro's brand, and its lack of presence in other cities meant the restaurant's unique offerings remained a local secret rather than a recognized brand.

Eventually, as Marco aged and became less able to handle the physical demands of restaurant work, the business's future came into question. Without a scalable model or a trained team to uphold the bistro's standards, the restaurant couldn't expand or evolve beyond its single location. Chef Marco's Bistro remained beloved but small, missing out on the potential to grow into a successful regional or even national brand. This example illustrates how being too focused on operations can prevent a business from achieving scalable growth. By not building a model that others could replicate, Chef Marco's Bistro ultimately lost out on significant opportunities for expansion and brand recognition.

### *4. The Manufacturer That Failed to Innovate:*

Johnson Fabrications, a family-owned manufacturing company, had been producing high-quality metal components for the automotive industry for over 40 years. Known for its reliable products and meticulous quality control, the company maintained long-standing relationships with several key clients. When Charlie Johnson took over the business from his parents, he continued their hands-on approach, overseeing production lines, personally inspecting batches for quality, and managing everyday operations. He valued the company's traditional methods, believing they were the backbone of its success.

However, as the manufacturing industry evolved, new technologies and production methods began reshaping the landscape:

- Automation and Robotics: Competitors started integrating automated production lines and robotic machinery, reducing labor costs and increasing production speed. By contrast, Johnson Fabrications continued with largely manual processes, which were slower and costlier to maintain. Automation could have streamlined the company's operations, allowing it to produce more at a lower

cost, but Charlie was hesitant, fearing it would compromise quality.
- Advanced Materials and Lightweight Components: As the automotive industry shifted towards fuel efficiency, there was a growing demand for lightweight materials, such as aluminum alloys and composites. Competitors invested in R&D and adapted to produce lighter, more durable components. Johnson Fabrications, however, stuck with its traditional metal materials and manufacturing methods, failing to meet the changing needs of the market.
- Digital Quality Control and Predictive Maintenance: Many manufacturers began using digital sensors and AI-driven quality control systems to detect flaws in real time and perform predictive maintenance, which reduced downtime. Charlie relied on manual inspections and traditional maintenance schedules, which were both time-consuming and prone to human error. Digital systems could have enhanced efficiency and quality, but he felt his personal oversight was more reliable.

Consequences: Over the next decade, Johnson Fabrications began losing contracts to competitors who could offer faster, cheaper, and more innovative solutions. The company's costs remained high, and its production capabilities fell behind industry standards. Clients who once valued Johnson Fabrications for its quality now sought out manufacturers with advanced materials and faster turnaround times. By refusing to adapt, Charlie watched as the company's revenue dropped by 40 percent, and the business struggled to attract new clients in an industry increasingly focused on innovation.

Eventually, Charlie was forced to downsize the company, cutting back on production lines and laying off workers. With an outdated production model and fewer clients, Johnson Fabrications was no longer competitive in the modern manufacturing landscape. The lack of investment in innovation left it unable to meet evolving market demands, putting its once-solid reputation at risk. This example illustrates how a reluctance to innovate and adapt to new technologies can cause even a successful manufacturer to lose its competitive edge. Without a forward-thinking approach, Johnson Fabrications ultimately fell behind, proving that in a changing industry, tradition alone cannot sustain growth.

## *5. The Consulting Firm That Didn't Adapt:*

Insight Advisors, a boutique consulting firm specializing in strategic planning for healthcare providers, had built a strong reputation over two decades. Known for its personalized service and deep industry knowledge, the firm catered to a loyal client base of small to mid-sized clinics and medical practices. The founder, Laura, was the face of the firm – she personally handled client relationships, led project management, and was deeply involved in the consulting work itself. Clients valued her expertise, and she prided herself on the customized solutions she offered based on years of industry experience.

However, as the consulting industry evolved, so did client expectations:

- Digital Tools for Client Engagement: Larger consulting firms began offering digital dashboards that allowed clients to track project progress, receive real-time insights, and communicate directly with consultants. These tools provided transparency and convenience, enabling clients to stay engaged throughout the consulting process. Insight Advisors, however, relied on traditional methods – client updates were given in meetings or via email, and project tracking was done manually. Without a digital platform, Laura's clients had

limited visibility into project timelines and deliverables.
- Data-Driven Insights and Predictive Analytics: Competitors introduced data analytics and AI tools to help clients make more informed, evidence-based decisions. These firms offered insights into industry trends, patient behavior, and operational benchmarks, using predictive analytics to forecast patient flow and optimize resource allocation. Insight Advisors continued to rely on Laura's expertise and past experiences, but without data-driven tools, the firm struggled to provide the same level of actionable, forward-looking insights.
- Virtual Consultations and Remote Collaboration: As remote work became the norm, other firms began offering virtual consultation sessions and online workshops that allowed clients to access services without needing to meet in person. Laura preferred in-person meetings, viewing them as a cornerstone of her personalized service. However, clients increasingly sought the flexibility of virtual consulting, especially as healthcare practices became busier. Without a robust online setup, Insight Advisors missed out on a growing segment of clients who preferred remote services.

Consequences: Within a few years, Insight Advisors began to lose clients to larger, more tech-savvy firms that could offer a more streamlined and transparent consulting experience. Clients who once valued the firm's personalized approach started choosing firms that could provide both personalization and digital convenience. As competitors expanded their digital capabilities, Insight Advisors struggled to keep up, with Laura's manual processes and lack of digital tools seen as outdated.

Revenue began to decline, and Laura faced mounting

pressure to modernize the firm's approach. However, the cost and time required to adopt digital tools, train staff, and shift to data-driven methods seemed daunting, and Insight Advisors was left behind. Eventually, Laura was forced to consider merging with a larger firm, losing the independence she had valued for years. This example illustrates how failing to adapt to industry-wide shifts can make a boutique consulting firm less competitive. By sticking with traditional methods and overlooking the benefits of digital tools, Insight Advisors lost clients to firms that could blend expertise with technology, offering a more comprehensive and efficient consulting experience.

## Why the Distinction Matters: The Impact on Business Growth and Success

The distinction between being an entrepreneur and an operator is not just academic; it has real, tangible effects on the success and growth of a business. When a business owner acts as an operator, they may ensure that the business runs smoothly, but they also risk stagnation. Without a focus on growth, innovation, and long-term strategy, the business may survive, but it won't thrive.

In contrast, when a business owner embraces the role of an entrepreneur, they are positioning their business for success. Entrepreneurs are forward-thinking, always looking for ways to expand and innovate. They understand that to grow, they must take risks, embrace change, and constantly seek out new opportunities. This proactive approach leads to increased revenue, profitability, and the long-term sustainability of the business.

Moreover, the entrepreneurial approach fosters a culture of innovation within the company. Employees are encouraged to think creatively and contribute ideas that can drive the business forward. This not only leads to new products, services, and markets but also creates a more engaged and motivated workforce.

The following specific metrics and numbers powerfully

illustrate the impact of shifting from an operator mindset to an entrepreneurial one. The Small Business That Accelerated Growth: BrightLeaf Packaging, a small business specializing in eco-friendly packaging solutions, had been operating steadily for a decade. Known for its high-quality, sustainable materials and excellent customer service, the company grew at a consistent, if modest, rate of about 5 percent per year. The founder, Lisa, managed the business conservatively, focusing on maintaining customer loyalty and delivering quality products. However, as the market for sustainable packaging expanded, BrightLeaf faced increasing competition from larger companies with more advanced technology and aggressive marketing strategies.

Recognizing the need for change, Lisa decided to adopt a visionary leadership strategy that would transform BrightLeaf from a small, steady-growth business into a competitive, rapidly growing player. She implemented three major shifts:

- Investment in AI and Automation: Lisa invested in AI-driven demand forecasting and inventory management tools to predict customer needs and streamline production. The company also automated its packaging process, increasing production speed and reducing costs. These changes allowed BrightLeaf to respond to orders faster and handle a larger volume without sacrificing quality. Automation reduced waste and enabled better resource allocation, which helped improve the company's profit margins.
- Enhanced Market Expansion Strategy: Previously, BrightLeaf's customer base was largely local and limited to small businesses. Lisa created a dedicated sales and marketing team tasked with identifying and targeting new markets, including larger companies and international clients. She developed an online platform that showcased

BrightLeaf's offerings, allowing for easier ordering and attracting clients from outside the local area. A digital marketing campaign focused on sustainability and quality brought in a steady stream of new customers.
- Data-Driven Customer Insights: By implementing customer relationship management (CRM) software with AI capabilities, Lisa's team could analyze customer buying patterns and tailor products and services to meet specific client needs. The CRM tool enabled BrightLeaf to develop customized packaging solutions, enhancing customer loyalty and creating opportunities for upselling and cross-selling. This personalized approach not only improved customer satisfaction but also boosted repeat business.

Results: Within two years of adopting these changes, BrightLeaf's annual revenue growth rate jumped from 5 percent to 20 percent. The automation and AI tools reduced operational costs by 15 percent, and the expanded market strategy brought in new clients from different regions and industries, significantly increasing BrightLeaf's market share. By positioning itself as a technologically advanced, customer-centric company, BrightLeaf not only retained its loyal customer base but also attracted larger clients interested in scalable, sustainable packaging solutions.

This visionary approach helped BrightLeaf become a leader in the eco-friendly packaging industry, proving that a small business can achieve significant growth by investing in technology, expanding its market reach, and focusing on customer insights.

Improving Customer Retention and Satisfaction through Strategic Focus

Gemini Fitness, a mid-sized gym and wellness center, had a solid customer base but struggled with retention and satisfaction. Membership renewal rates were around 70 percent, with frequent complaints about long wait times for equipment, inconsistent class schedules, and difficulty getting personalized attention from trainers. The owner, Jamie, spent most of her time managing day-to-day operations, including staffing, scheduling, and inventory management, which left little time to address these deeper issues impacting customer experience.

Recognizing the need for change, Jamie decided to step back from daily tasks and adopt a strategic approach focused on customer retention and satisfaction. She implemented three major initiatives:

1. Enhanced Member Onboarding and Support: Jamie redesigned the member onboarding process to be more engaging and personalized. New members were paired with a fitness coach who helped them set achievable goals, introduced them to the facility, and scheduled a complimentary check-in every few months. This personal touch created stronger initial connections and set a positive tone for their experience.

2. Investing in Digital Convenience: Jamie introduced a user-friendly mobile app that allowed members to easily reserve equipment, schedule classes, and receive reminders for personal training sessions. The app provided real-time updates on class availability and gym capacity, reducing wait times and improving convenience. Feedback channels were also added to the app, allowing members to share their opinions and suggestions instantly, which created a sense of involvement and responsiveness.

3. Consistent, High-Quality Member Engagement: Jamie established a customer experience team that focused on consistent communication with members. The team regularly reached out to check on members' progress, offered special promotions, and sought feedback on their experience. The gym also launched a loyalty program that

rewarded long-term members with perks like free training sessions and discounts on wellness products, adding value for committed customers.

Results: Within a year of implementing these changes, Gemini Fitness saw its customer retention rate increase from 70 percent to 90 percent. The enhanced customer experience and personalized approach improved satisfaction rates significantly, with surveys showing a 25 percent increase in customer satisfaction. Members frequently mentioned feeling valued and appreciated, and the app's convenience features were particularly popular, helping to address prior frustrations around scheduling and availability.

By focusing on customer experience, Gemini Fitness not only boosted loyalty and satisfaction but also created a community-centered environment that attracted referrals and new memberships. Jamie's shift from operational management to strategic customer engagement proved essential in transforming Gemini Fitness from a typical gym into a preferred wellness destination.

Operational Efficiency Gains Through Technology Adoption: ClearView Financial, a financial advisory firm, managed a wide range of client accounts, from personal investments to retirement planning. However, as the firm grew, its team became bogged down by time-consuming manual tasks, including data entry, document preparation, and report generation. Employees were spending a significant portion of their day on repetitive administrative work, limiting their capacity for high-value activities such as client consultations, strategy sessions, and business development.

To address these challenges, ClearView's leadership decided to invest in automation and digital tools to streamline operations and improve efficiency. They implemented three key initiatives:

1. Automated Data Entry and Document Processing: The firm adopted a digital document management system with optical character

recognition (OCR) technology, which automatically scanned, processed, and stored client documents. This reduced the need for manual data entry and document filing, saving the team hours each day. The system also automatically flagged documents that required follow-up, ensuring nothing was missed.
2. Client Report Generation with AI-Powered Software: ClearView implemented AI-powered software to generate personalized client reports with just a few clicks. What once required hours of gathering data, running calculations, and formatting documents was now accomplished in minutes. The software created detailed, customized reports that advisors could easily review and discuss with clients.
3. Automated Scheduling and Client Communication: The firm introduced an automated scheduling tool that allowed clients to book consultations online. This tool integrated with the advisors' calendars, reducing the back-and-forth often required to schedule meetings. ClearView also set up automated email reminders and follow-ups for client appointments, keeping communication consistent and professional without manual effort.

Results: Within six months, ClearView achieved notable operational efficiency gains:

- 50 percent Reduction in Time Spent on Manual Processes: Automation reduced the time spent on administrative tasks by half, significantly decreasing the burden on employees. Document processing, report generation, and scheduling, once highly manual, became streamlined and required minimal human intervention.
- 30 percent Increase in Employee Capacity for

High-Value Activities: Freed from repetitive tasks, advisors could dedicate more time to building client relationships, developing new financial strategies, and prospecting for new clients. This shift led to higher engagement and better outcomes for clients, enhancing the firm's reputation.

- 15 percent Reduction in Operational Costs: With increased productivity and a reduction in manual work, ClearView's operational costs decreased by 15 percent. Fewer resources were needed to manage existing workloads, allowing the firm to reallocate funds toward client service improvements and strategic growth initiatives.

By leveraging automation, ClearView Financial transformed its operations, achieving higher productivity, reduced costs, and more capacity for client-centered work. This strategic investment in technology positioned the firm to scale effectively, demonstrating how technology adoption can drive both efficiency and growth in a competitive industry. This case study shows the impact of technology on operational efficiency and the cascading benefits of freeing up employees for high-value tasks.

## Margin Increase by Focusing on Core Business Goals

Silverline Solutions, a mid-sized IT services firm, has developed a reputation for tackling a wide variety of client requests, from routine IT support to complex software integrations. While this broad service offering brought in a steady stream of projects, it also stretched the company thin, often leading to time-consuming, low-margin work. The owner, David, felt overwhelmed by the operational details of managing such a varied client base and frequently found himself "stuck" handling minor issues that detracted from the company's more profitable services.

Realizing the need to focus on growth rather than just survival, David adopted an entrepreneurial mindset. He embarked on a strategic shift to narrow Silverline's focus and prioritize high-margin services. His approach included three main steps:

1. Analyzing Profitability by Service Type: David conducted a thorough review of the company's financials, examining profit margins for each type of service. He discovered that complex software integration projects had the highest profit margins, while routine IT support was labor-intensive, generating much lower returns. Armed with these insights, David decided to phase out low-margin offerings and concentrate on integration services, which required specialized skills and had fewer competitors.
2. Realigning Resources to Core Services: To support the shift, David reorganized the team, assigning more staff to the software integration division and upskilling employees to meet the specific demands of these projects. He also invested in targeted training programs, ensuring his team had the advanced expertise needed for high-margin projects. By consolidating resources around core services, Silverline became known as a specialist in integration rather than a general IT provider.
3. Strategic Marketing and Positioning: David launched a marketing campaign to reposition Silverline as a go-to expert for complex software integrations, targeting industries that required specialized solutions, such as healthcare and finance. He focused on building relationships with key players in these sectors, creating a network of referral partners who could direct clients needing specific expertise. This strategy helped attract higher-value clients willing to pay a premium for Silverline's services.

Results: Over the next two years, this focused strategy transformed Silverline's financial performance:

- Increased Profit Margin from 10 percent to 18 percent: By phasing out low-margin services and concentrating on profitable integration projects, Silverline's profit margin rose from 10 percent to 18 percent. The company's streamlined offerings allowed it to concentrate on fewer, higher-value projects, resulting in more efficient operations and higher returns.
- Improved Team Morale and Expertise: With a clear focus and specialized training, employees felt more confident and engaged. They were no longer stretched thin across low-value tasks, allowing them to deliver higher-quality results in their specialized area.
- Enhanced Market Positioning: As Silverline became known for its expertise in software integrations, the firm attracted more clients in need of its high-margin services, creating a positive feedback loop that reinforced its position as a leader in its niche.

This strategic realignment helped David transition from a business operator bogged down by day-to-day tasks to a visionary leader focused on growth. By narrowing Silverline's scope and investing in its core strengths, he not only increased the company's profitability but also established a sustainable, scalable model for future success. This case study demonstrates the power of focusing on core business goals to improve profit margins, achieve operational efficiency, and strengthen market positioning.

## Time Savings in Strategic Decision-Making Through AI Analytics

GreenTech Materials, a supplier of eco-friendly building materials, had been facing increasing competition in a rapidly evolving market. In the past, its leadership team spent significant time gathering data manually and analyzing trends before making strategic decisions. The process was time-consuming, often resulting in reactive rather than proactive measures, as it took weeks to gather insights, interpret them, and decide on the best course of action.

To improve agility and stay ahead of competitors, GreenTech adopted an AI-based analytics platform capable of processing large volumes of data in real time. The platform was integrated with GreenTech's sales, customer feedback, and market trend databases, providing instant insights that were previously labor-intensive to obtain. The impact of this technology was transformative:

1. Real-Time Market Insights: The AI platform analyzed market trends continuously, identifying shifts in customer preferences, emerging material demands, and competitor activities. What once required days of analysis by the team could now be reviewed in minutes, allowing leadership to make decisions based on the most current data available.
2. Predictive Analytics for Demand Forecasting: The platform's AI-driven predictive models helped GreenTech anticipate changes in demand. By forecasting seasonal and regional material needs, the company was able to adjust its inventory and production schedules proactively, ensuring it could meet customer demands without delays or overproduction. Previously, such forecasting required extensive data gathering and manual calculations, but the AI solution streamlined this to an automated process.
3. Enhanced Scenario Analysis: Leadership used the AI system to run "what-if" scenarios, simulating outcomes of various strategic moves, such as expanding into a new region or introducing a new product line. The AI's ability to model these

scenarios quickly allowed the team to evaluate potential risks and benefits more efficiently than with manual scenario planning.

Results: After implementing AI-based analytics, GreenTech saw a 40 percent reduction in the time needed for strategic decision-making. This time savings enabled the leadership team to shift from reactive responses to proactive market moves. With faster insights and the ability to make data-driven decisions in real-time, GreenTech was able to:

- Launch new products more quickly in response to market demands, enhancing its competitive advantage.
- Respond to shifts in customer preferences ahead of competitors, increasing customer satisfaction and loyalty.
- Allocate resources and adjust strategies swiftly, improving operational efficiency and reducing costs related to overstocking or supply delays.

By leveraging AI-based analytics, GreenTech Materials transformed its approach to strategic decision-making, becoming a faster, more agile organization that could lead in a competitive market rather than simply react to it. This proactive stance positioned the company for long-term growth and resilience in an industry where timely decisions are key. This example highlights how AI-based analytics can drive time savings in strategic decision-making, enabling a company to respond faster and more effectively to market changes.

## Employee Engagement and Retention Improvement through Vision Alignment

Riviera Apparel, a mid-sized clothing brand, had always valued its creative team and sought to foster a collaborative environment. However, as the company grew, employees began to feel disconnected from the brand's mission, viewing their roles as tasks rather than meaningful contributions to a larger purpose. This lack of engagement led to declining morale, with employee engagement scores falling and annual turnover reaching 20 percent. Recognizing the need for change, the company's leadership decided to engage employees in its entrepreneurial vision and innovation strategy.

Riviera Apparel implemented three key initiatives to connect employees with the brand's purpose and innovation efforts:

1. Innovation and Idea-Sharing Platforms: The company introduced an internal platform where employees could submit and vote on new product ideas, designs, or process improvements. By involving staff in brainstorming sessions and encouraging them to contribute ideas, Riviera Apparel made every employee feel like a vital part of the company's growth. Top ideas were recognized, and some were developed into actual products or processes, creating a tangible connection between employee input and company outcomes.
2. Cross-Department Innovation Workshops: Riviera Apparel organized quarterly workshops that brought together employees from different departments – design, marketing, operations, and sales – to collaborate on new initiatives. These sessions allowed employees to step outside their day-to-day roles and think strategically about the company's goals, building a shared understanding of Riviera's mission and future direction. Leaders encouraged open dialogue, ensuring that each voice was valued.
3. Recognition and Career Growth Opportunities: To reinforce a sense of purpose and growth, Riviera Apparel implemented a formal recognition program, celebrating employees who contributed to the company's vision through innovation and

initiative. Employees who participated in or led successful projects were rewarded with professional development opportunities, such as attending industry conferences or receiving mentorship for career advancement.

Results: Within a year of implementing these initiatives, Riviera Apparel saw significant improvements:

- 25 percent Improvement in Employee Engagement Scores: Surveys showed that employees felt more connected to the company's vision and valued as part of its journey. The opportunity to contribute ideas and see them come to life created a sense of ownership and pride among the team.
- 10 percent Reduction in Annual Turnover: By fostering a culture of inclusion, purpose, and innovation, Riviera Apparel reduced turnover, particularly among high-performing employees who appreciated the company's commitment to their growth. The improved retention rate saved the company recruitment and training costs and helped preserve its skilled workforce.

Enhanced Innovation Pipeline: Engaged employees generated a steady stream of fresh ideas and product concepts, some of which turned into best-selling items and improved processes. This influx of innovation further reinforced the company's competitive edge and highlighted the value of employee contributions.

By engaging employees in its entrepreneurial vision and creating a culture that valued their ideas, Riviera Apparel transformed its workforce into active partners in its mission. The resulting increase in engagement and reduction in turnover positioned the company for sustained growth, with a team that felt both valued and invested in the brand's success. This example shows the powerful impact of involving employees in a company's vision and innovation strategy, highlighting how such engagement can boost retention and contribute to overall business success.

## Employee Engagement and Retention Improvement

In the long run, the distinction between being an entrepreneur and an operator can be the difference between a business that simply survives and one that truly thrives. These metrics demonstrate tangible results that come from transitioning from a traditional business operator mindset to a more entrepreneurial, growth-oriented approach. By understanding this distinction and adopting the entrepreneurial mindset, you can unlock your full potential, driving growth, innovation, and long-term success for your business. Tomorrow morning, track every task you do. Are you leading your business toward growth, or are you just keeping the lights on? The choice – and the consequences – are yours.

# CHAPTER 2:
# UNDERSTANDING THE BUSINESS YOU'RE IN

*"If you can dream it, you can do it."*

– Walt Disney

As the matriarch of a family-owned business, I have had the unique privilege of witnessing the evolution of our company from its inception to its current state. I've learned firsthand what separates visionary leaders from day-to-day operators.

Our journey, like that of many family businesses, has been one of growth, transition, and the continuous effort to build a legacy that transcends generations.

In the early years of our business, my husband Stephen was one of the founders, and he played an active role in the company. Like many founders, he was deeply involved in every aspect of the company. However, as the business grew, we realized that his role needed to change. To truly build something lasting – something that could be passed on to future generations – we needed to transition out of the day-to-day operations and focus on strategic leadership.

This decision marked a significant shift, not only for us but also for the future of our business. Our family was growing, and we wanted to create a legacy that could continue with our children. Our oldest son, Michael, had always shown a keen interest in the business and had a natural ability to see things from a fresh, modern perspective. It became clear that he was the right person to take the helm as CEO and lead the company into its next phase of growth.

## The Next Generation: Innovation and AI

With our son in the CEO role, our family business underwent a transformation. One of the most critical changes he implemented was integrating AI technology to streamline operations and enhance decision-making processes. This marked the beginning of a new era for our company – one in which technology played a central role in driving growth and efficiency. While we had built the foundation, Michael was now taking it to the next level, bringing innovation and a forward-thinking approach to the table. Under Michael's leadership, our AI integration will reduce operational costs by 10 percent and increase productivity by 20 percent, proving that letting go of control doesn't mean losing it.

The transition from one generation to the next is never without challenges, but it's also an opportunity for growth and renewal. By embracing AI and other emerging technologies, our son has been able to position the business for long-term success, ensuring that our family's legacy continues to thrive in a rapidly changing world. Having guided numerous families through succession planning in my first book, *Family Business Legacy,* I've seen how the operator-to-entrepreneur transition can make or break generational wealth.

In that book, I discussed the importance of creating a strong foundation based on values, trust, and resilience. Now, I want to highlight how transitioning leadership and embracing innovation are just as critical in ensuring the continued growth and sustainability of the business.

Our family's experience can serve as a guide for other family businesses facing similar challenges. The lessons we have learned about trusting the next generation and leveraging technology are applicable to any business looking to create a lasting legacy.

## The Universal Principles of Leadership from our Family Business

While the transition within our family-owned business is a powerful example of how smaller, more intimate operations can navigate leadership changes and embrace innovation, this same principle holds true for larger organizations. In the following sections, we will explore how several large-sized companies have successfully executed similar transformations on a much broader scale. These examples will show that whether you're running a small family-owned business or a global enterprise, the shift from operator to entrepreneur and the strategic use of technology are vital to continued growth and success.

By examining the strategies these larger companies employed, you'll see how the concepts discussed earlier can be applied universally, proving that the path to sustainable growth and visionary leadership is not bound by the size of the business but by the willingness to embrace change and innovation.

## The Illusion of Control: Common Misconceptions Entrepreneurs Have About Their Business Roles

Many entrepreneurs fall into the trap of believing that by handling every aspect of their business, they maintain control and ensure success. This belief is rooted in the illusion of control – the idea that being deeply involved in every task will guarantee that everything runs smoothly. While it's true that attention to detail is important, this mindset can lead to micromanagement and a loss of focus on what truly matters: growing the business.

One of the most common misconceptions is that the more involved an entrepreneur is in the day-to-day operations, the better off the business will be. This hands-on approach can feel satisfying because it gives the entrepreneur a sense of control and accomplishment.

MARIA L. ELLIS

## When Hands-On Becomes a Hindrance

While this hands-on approach is crucial in the initial phases, it can rapidly transform into an obstacle as your business expands, limiting your ability to think strategically and seize new opportunities for growth. For example, our own growing media aggregator initially thrived on its founders' hands-on approach. The founders were deeply involved in selecting and curating content sources, managing client relationships, and personally reviewing the distribution processes. This close involvement helped the company establish a reputation for high-quality, reliable content curation and personalized customer service, which attracted a loyal client base of publishers and media outlets.

However, as the company expanded, this hands-on approach started to limit the business's potential.

- Missed Technology Integration Opportunities: While the founders focused on manually curating content and troubleshooting client requests, competitors began integrating AI-driven algorithms for content recommendations, personalization, and data analytics. These tools provided faster, more customized news feeds that clients increasingly preferred. The founders had considered adopting similar technologies but didn't have the time to implement them. As a result, the company began losing ground to tech-savvy competitors offering innovative solutions that were now industry standards.
- Scaling Challenges and Client Dissatisfaction: With the founders personally involved in approving content sources and handling client communications, the company struggled to onboard new clients quickly. Some clients even took their business to other aggregators who could respond faster. The founders' hands-on approach, once a strength, now created bottlenecks in scaling the

company's client base and content variety.
- Team Morale and Innovation Stagnation: The company eventually brought on a small team to assist with client relations and content management. However, this needs to oversee every detail left employees feeling underutilized and disengaged. Several team members suggested automating processes or expanding into new media formats, like podcasts or video clips, to diversify the company's offerings. The founders' resistance to let go of control, however, stifled innovation, and employees grew frustrated with the lack of growth opportunities.

Consequences: As a result, the company found itself trapped in its current state. Growth slowed, and client retention declined as competitors offered faster, more innovative services. The company was struggling to keep up in an industry where speed, customization, and advanced technology were becoming the norm.

Realizing his hands-on approach was now holding the business back, the founders finally decided to step back from day-to-day tasks. They hired a technology lead to implement AI-driven content curation and a customer success manager to ensure clients received timely, quality service. With the team empowered, the founders could now focus on strategic growth opportunities, such as expanding content sources, exploring new media formats, and establishing partnerships with key industry players.

This shift transformed the company into an agile, innovative media aggregator, positioned to adapt to changing industry demands and deliver higher-value services to clients. By letting go of the illusion of control, the founders were able to focus on the big picture, ensuring the company's continued growth and success. This example demonstrates how a hands-on approach in a news and media aggregator can initially build a strong foundation but ultimately become a barrier to innovation, scalability, and strategic growth.

Another misconception is that delegating tasks means losing control. Many entrepreneurs fear that if they delegate, the quality of work will suffer, or that important tasks will not be completed to their standards. This fear can lead to burnout and stifle the business's growth potential. In reality, effective delegation is a hallmark of successful leadership. It allows entrepreneurs to focus on high-level decisions and strategic initiatives while empowering their team to take ownership of their roles.

Understanding that true control comes from leading, not managing, is a crucial step for entrepreneurs. It's about recognizing that their value lies in their ability to guide the business toward growth and innovation, not in overseeing every detail.

## Seeing the Bigger Picture: Are You Operating or Truly Leading?

To move from the role of an operator to that of a true leader, entrepreneurs must learn to see the bigger picture. This involves stepping back from daily operations and assessing whether their actions are contributing to the long-term success of the business.

One way to determine if you are operating or truly leading your business is to evaluate where you spend most of your time. If most of your day is consumed with putting out fires, managing employee issues, or handling routine tasks, you are likely operating rather than leading. While these tasks are important, they should not dominate your time. Instead, a significant portion of your time should be dedicated to strategic planning, exploring new opportunities, and driving the business forward.

Another indicator is your decision-making process. Leaders make decisions based on long-term goals and the overall vision for the company. They consider how each decision aligns with the business's mission and how it will impact future growth. Operators, on the other hand, tend to make decisions based on immediate needs and short-term solutions. While these decisions may solve problems in the moment, they often fail to contribute to the bigger picture.

To truly lead your business, you need to cultivate a mindset that prioritizes growth and innovation over routine operations. This means trusting your team to handle the day-to-day tasks while you focus on guiding the business toward its future.

## Key Metrics and Turning Points in the Shift from Operator to Leader

The following example, with specific metrics and turning points, shows how a shift from operational focus to strategic leadership can drive substantial growth, client satisfaction, and employee engagement in a growing company.

As the company grew, the founders remained deeply involved in every aspect of the business – from selecting and curating content sources to personally managing client relationships. Initially, this hands-on approach ensured high standards, helping the company build a strong reputation in the niche media aggregation market. However, as the business expanded, the company faced pivotal challenges and metrics that made it clear they needed to transition from operator to visionary leader.

- Revenue Plateau and Stagnant Client Growth: Despite the company's solid foundation, growth began to stall. Annual revenue growth had slowed to 5 percent, down from the 20 percent the company had achieved in its early years. Additionally, new client onboarding times had doubled, from two weeks to a month, as the company struggled to keep up with personally managing each account. This delay caused frustration for both the team and clients, leading to increased complaints and a missed opportunity to capture new clients. At this point, Alex realized his hands-on approach was limiting the company's potential to scale.

- Declining Client Retention Rate: The company's client retention rate dropped from 92 percent to 85 percent over 18 months. While subtle, this shift was a warning sign. Clients noted slower response times and limited customization compared to competitors who had adopted AI and automation for real-time content personalization. Clients seeking faster, more responsive services started to explore alternative providers. Seeing this decline in retention, the founders understood that focusing solely on operational tasks was preventing them from addressing bigger strategic needs – like adopting technology to deliver a competitive client experience.
- Employee Turnover and Innovation Bottlenecks: The company's employees began voicing concerns about the lack of autonomy and growth. Three key team members left over the course of a year, citing limited decision-making power and opportunities for innovation. The team had proposed implementing automation for client management and content recommendations, but the founders' reluctance to delegate delayed progress. This turnover created a bottleneck, impacting productivity and morale. Realizing his control was holding back both his team and the company's potential, the founders knew it was time to empower others and trust them with more responsibility.
- Direct Competitor Overtakes in Market Share: The company's main competitor, which had invested in AI-driven content curation and predictive analytics, surpassed the company in market share for the first time. The competitor's agile response to client needs and innovative features led to a 15 percent increase in their customer base, which included clients that the company had

previously served. This turning point was a wake-up call, and to keep the company competitive, the founders needed to move away from day-to-day operations and focus on strategic leadership.

The Shift to Leadership: These metrics and turning points made it clear that the founders' operational focus was limiting the company's potential. The founders decided to make a decisive shift:

- Hiring a new CEO and a new Chief Technology Officer: The founders hired a new CEO and a new CTO to spearhead the adoption of AI and automation in content curation. This allowed the company to offer real-time personalization, which boosted client satisfaction and retention.
- Empowering a Client Success Team: The founders established a client success team dedicated to managing relationships, handling inquiries, and tracking satisfaction metrics. This move reduced client onboarding time by 50 percent and freed the founders to focus on growth and innovation.
- Investing in Employee Training and Autonomy: The founders implemented a training program for employees to develop new skills and take on leadership roles within their departments. With clear goals, the team felt more engaged and motivated, which stabilized turnover and renewed morale.

Results: Within two years of making these changes, the company saw a dramatic turnaround:

- Revenue Growth Rebound: Annual revenue growth rebounded to 18 percent as the business scaled more efficiently, driven by the adoption of AI-driven processes.
- Client Retention Increased: The client retention rate rose from 85 percent back up to 93 percent, as the company could now meet and exceed client expectations with personalized, data-driven

content services.
- Employee Satisfaction and Productivity: Employee satisfaction scores rose by 30 percent, with team members feeling more empowered and trusted. Productivity increased, and turnover stabilized, creating a stronger, more cohesive team.

Through these changes, the founders learned that stepping back from operational control and adopting a strategic, visionary leadership role allowed the company to thrive in an increasingly competitive industry. The illusion of control had been holding back the company's potential, but by focusing on growth and empowering their team, the founders transformed the company into a more agile, scalable, and competitive business.

## The Importance of Understanding Your Business: A Story of Success and Failure

Understanding the true nature of your business is crucial to its success. Many entrepreneurs start with a clear vision of what their business is, only to find that the market, technology, and customer needs evolve in ways they didn't anticipate. The ability to recognize and adapt to these changes can mean the difference between thriving and failing. To illustrate this point, let's explore two stories: one of success and one of failure – both driven by the entrepreneurs' understanding (or lack thereof) of the business they were truly in.

## Key Takeaways: Understanding the Business You're In

These case studies highlight the critical importance of understanding the true nature of your business. Kodak and Blockbuster failed to recognize the broader value they provided and clung to outdated business models, ultimately leading to their decline. In contrast, Netflix and Fujifilm understood that their businesses were about more than just the products they originally offered. They recognized the need to adapt to changing technologies and market demands, leading to their continued success.

As an entrepreneur, it's essential to continually assess the business you're in, beyond the immediate products or services you offer. Ask yourself what value you're truly providing to your customers, how the market is evolving, and what technological advancements could disrupt or enhance your business. By staying adaptable and keeping the bigger picture in mind, you can position your business for long-term growth and success, avoiding the pitfalls of those who failed to see beyond their initial offerings.

# CHAPTER 3:
# THE BUSINESS YOU SHOULD BE IN

*"Risk more than others think is safe.*
*Dream more than others think is practical."*
*— Howard Schultz*

Transitioning from a business operator to a visionary entrepreneur is one of the most significant steps you can take for the long-term success of your business. The journey ahead is not just about learning new strategies – it's about adopting a new mindset and understanding your role as a leader. In other words, the single greatest factor holding your business back is you – specifically, your role as an operator rather than a visionary entrepreneur. But we're going to change that. Here's how. Let me guide you through the essential lessons in each chapter of this book, highlighting why these insights are vital for overcoming the challenges you face as a business owner. Along the way, I'll share success stories that illustrate how these concepts have been successfully applied in real-life situations, providing tangible examples to inspire and inform your journey. Finally, I'll offer practical advice on how to approach each chapter to maximize the value you gain from this book.

Let me guide you through the key lessons ahead.

## What You Will Learn in Each Chapter

- Chapter 4: Leveraging Technology for Growth Technology is one of the biggest enablers for entrepreneurs today. In this chapter, you will learn about the specific technologies that can help you scale your business, streamline operations, and automate processes. Without embracing technology, businesses risk falling behind, which is why this chapter is essential for any entrepreneur looking to stay competitive.

- Chapter 5: Scaling Your Business Growth isn't just about adding more customers or products; it's about scaling intelligently. This chapter outlines the steps you need to take to ensure your business can scale efficiently without compromising quality or customer satisfaction. Whether you're a small business owner or a CEO of a larger organization, understanding how to scale is vital for long-term success. From my experience working with both small business owners and CEOs of larger organizations, I have seen how understanding scalability directly impacts long-term success.
- Chapter 6: Building a Strong Leadership Team Your success as an entrepreneur isn't just about what you do – it's about the team you build. This chapter focuses on the importance of leadership and team development, ensuring you have the right people in place to help you achieve your vision. A strong team allows you to focus on high-level strategy while they handle the operational aspects.
- Chapter 7: The Entrepreneurial Mindset Here, we dive deep into the mindset shifts necessary for becoming a successful entrepreneur. This chapter explores how to cultivate resilience, creativity, and a future-focused approach. Without the right mindset, all the tools and strategies in the world won't help you reach your goals.
- Chapter 8: Lessons from Large-Scale Businesses:

In this chapter, we look at examples of large companies that have successfully transitioned from operator-driven management to visionary entrepreneurship. By understanding how larger businesses implement these changes, you'll gain insight into strategies that can be applied at any level of business.
- Chapters 9 and 10: The Final Push to Entrepreneurial Success: These final chapters will tie everything together, emphasizing the importance of taking action. You will learn how to avoid common pitfalls, stay adaptable, and continue growing even after you've made the transition from operator to entrepreneur.
- Chapters 11, 12, and 13: The final three chapters serve as both your guide and inspiration for leaders who wish to make their culture a cornerstone of visionary leadership and encourage leaders to see beyond profit, creating a legacy of impact that endures.

## Strategic Focus: Identifying the Actual Business You're In

Recognizing your business's core value proposition requires a strategic focus that goes beyond daily tasks and immediate concerns. It's about identifying the core value your business provides and how that value fits into the broader market.

I have found the Value Proposition Canvas to be an invaluable tool for helping business owners identify their true business focus. This framework helps you understand your customers' needs and how your business meets those needs. By focusing on the value you deliver, rather than the products or services you offer, you can gain a clearer understanding of your business's true purpose.

Another useful framework is the Business Model Canvas, which allows you to map out the key components of your business, including your value proposition, customer segments, revenue streams, and key partnerships. This exercise can help you see where your business fits in the market and how you can position yourself for growth.

Additionally, conducting a SWOT Analysis (Strengths, Weaknesses, Opportunities, Threats) can provide valuable insights into the internal and external factors that impact your business. By understanding these factors, you can develop strategies that leverage your strengths, mitigate your weaknesses, capitalize on opportunities, and protect against threats.

Finally, it's important to regularly review and update your Strategic Plan. This plan should outline your business's long-term goals and the steps you need to take to achieve them. It should be a living document that evolves as your business grows and the market changes.

By using these tools and frameworks, you can gain a deeper understanding of the business you're in and ensure that your efforts are aligned with your long-term vision. This strategic focus will enable you to lead your business with confidence, making decisions that drive growth and ensure sustained success.

As you can see, I am going to guide you through a process with tangible steps and recommendations to help you grow from operator to entrepreneur. But, before we do that, I want to share some case studies with you to illustrate the importance of adapting to change and anticipating trends.

## Case Studies: Successful Pivots and Expansions

The following case studies illustrate the importance of adapting to change and anticipating trends. Let's look at a couple of examples of companies that successfully pivoted or expanded into new areas to remain competitive.

### *Success Story 1: From Shop Floor to Strategic Leadership: A Manufacturer's Evolution*

As CEO of a $25 million metal fabrication company

with 50 employees, David had built what many would consider a successful business. However, like many business owners, David was stuck in the role of an operator. He was constantly troubleshooting issues on the production floor, overseeing orders, and managing his team. Despite the company's success, he felt exhausted and overwhelmed. He knew that if he didn't make a change, his business would plateau – and so would he.

After applying the strategies in this book, David realized that his biggest roadblock was his unwillingness to let go of operational control. He began by delegating critical tasks to his production manager, empowering his leadership team to make decisions without his constant input. David also invested in automation technology to streamline production processes, reducing errors and improving efficiency. The result? Within two years, David had expanded the company's capacity by 50 percent, entered new markets, and increased profitability by 35 percent. By transitioning from operator to entrepreneur, David could focus on big-picture strategy and growing his business, rather than micromanaging operations.

### *Success Story 2: From Operator to Entrepreneur*

Let me share with you the story of Rebecca, the owner of a mid-sized retail company who felt stuck in the day-to-day operations of her business. Rebecca was juggling inventory management, customer service, and marketing, and felt like she had hit a ceiling – her business couldn't grow beyond its current size without her being involved in every aspect.

After implementing strategic delegation and embracing automation, Rebecca made the decision to hire a strong leadership team and delegate the operational tasks that had consumed her time. She also embraced AI-powered inventory management systems that allowed her business to run more efficiently without her constant oversight. This freed up her time to focus on expanding the business, developing strategic partnerships, and growing her brand.

Within a year, Rebecca's business revenue had doubled, and she was no longer bogged down by the minutiae of running the business. She had transitioned from being an operator to a visionary entrepreneur, and her business was thriving as a result. Rebecca's story shows that it's not only possible to make this transition, but it can also unlock tremendous growth opportunities for your business.

## How to Get the Most Out of This Book

Through my years of guiding business owners through this transition, I've found these approaches most effective for implementing change.

1. Read in Order: Each chapter builds on the lessons of the previous one, so it's important to read them sequentially. The transition from operator to entrepreneur is a process, and each chapter represents a stage in that process.
2. Take Your Time: While it may be tempting to read through the book quickly, I recommend taking your time with each chapter. Reflect on the concepts and consider how they apply to your business. Journaling your thoughts and ideas after each chapter can help solidify your understanding and generate actionable insights.
3. Action Steps: Don't just read – take action. After each chapter, I encourage you to implement at least one strategy or piece of advice in your business. This will help you see real progress and keep you motivated throughout the journey.
4. Journal Your Journey: As you go through the book, I suggest keeping a journal to document your thoughts, ideas, and progress. This will help you track your transition from operator to entrepreneur and give you a clear view of how far you've come by the end of the book.

## Overarching Philosophy: Leadership, Innovation, and Adaptability

My research and experience have shown that entrepreneurial success consistently rests on three fundamental pillars: Leadership, Innovation, and Adaptability. Throughout every chapter, these principles will be woven into the lessons and strategies provided.

- Leadership: As an entrepreneur, you must lead with vision, not just manage with efficiency. By empowering others, you'll create a business that can grow and thrive without your constant involvement.
- Innovation: Embracing new technologies and ideas is essential to staying ahead in today's business world. Innovation is what will set you apart from your competition and ensure your business continues to grow.
- Adaptability: The ability to adapt to change is what will keep your business resilient in the face of challenges. The world of business is constantly evolving, and those who can pivot and adjust will find long-term success.

This chapter also emphasizes the need for entrepreneurs to remain agile and forward-thinking in their approach to business. By understanding the importance of adapting to change, anticipating trends, and being willing to innovate, entrepreneurs can ensure that their businesses remain relevant and competitive in an evolving marketplace. The case studies provide real-world examples of how successful companies have navigated these challenges and emerged stronger for it.

## Adapting to Change: The Evolution of Markets and Customer Needs

My research into market dynamics has shown that the

pace of change has increased exponentially; markets and customer needs are constantly evolving. What worked yesterday may not be effective tomorrow, and the ability to adapt is crucial for survival. The business you started with may not be the business you need to stay in if you want to remain competitive and relevant.

Adapting to change requires a keen understanding of the market dynamics that influence your industry. This means keeping a pulse on customer preferences, technological advancements, regulatory changes, and economic shifts. Customers' expectations are higher than ever, driven by the rapid development of technology and the increasing availability of choices. As a result, businesses must be agile and responsive to these changing demands.

In my work with successful entrepreneurs, those who thrive share one common practice: they continually assess their offerings and ask themselves whether their products or services still meet the needs of their target market. This may involve refining existing products, developing new ones, or even shifting the focus of the business entirely. It's about being proactive rather than reactive – anticipating changes before they occur and positioning your business to capitalize on new opportunities.

The key to adapting to change is maintaining a customer-centric approach. By staying attuned to what your customers want and need, you can ensure that your business evolves in a way that meets their expectations and keeps them loyal to your brand. This might involve investing in new technologies, expanding into new markets, or rethinking your value proposition.

## Foresight and Innovation: Anticipating Industry Trends

Successful entrepreneurs are those who not only respond to changes in the market but also anticipate them. Foresight and innovation are critical components of this approach. By keeping an eye on emerging trends and technological advancements, entrepreneurs can position their businesses to take advantage of new opportunities and avoid being left behind.

Throughout my decades in business, I have learned that foresight requires more than just market awareness; it demands a systematic approach to analyzing industry trends. Grounding theory in experience, economic shifts, and technological advancements will shape the future of your business. This means regularly conducting market research, attending industry conferences, and networking with other business leaders to stay informed about what's on the horizon.

Innovation, on the other hand, is about turning these insights into action. It's not enough to simply recognize a trend; you must also be willing to innovate and adapt your business model to leverage these changes. This might involve developing new products or services, exploring new markets, or adopting new technologies that can streamline operations or enhance customer experience.

One of the biggest challenges entrepreneurs face is the fear of change. It's easy to become comfortable with the status quo, especially if your business is currently successful. However, in today's rapidly changing business landscape, complacency can be dangerous. Entrepreneurs must be willing to embrace change, take calculated risks, and invest in innovation to stay ahead of the competition.

## The Critical Importance of Adapting to Change

These case studies illustrate the dire consequences that can result from a failure to adapt to change. Whether it's technological advancements, shifts in consumer behavior, or the emergence of new business models, change is inevitable in every industry. Businesses that fail to recognize and respond to these changes are at risk of losing their competitive edge, market share, and ultimately, their very existence. On the other hand, companies like Amazon, Apple, and Netflix that were proactive in adapting to change, embraced innovation, and invested in new technologies are the ones that thrive in the long term. Understanding the business you're truly in means recognizing the need for evolution and being willing to take bold steps to stay ahead of the curve. The business you start with may not be the business you should stay in, and the ability to adapt is key to ensuring continued growth and success.

This book is a comprehensive guide for entrepreneurs who are ready to take their business to the next level by leveraging vision, technology, leadership, and well-being. It's a roadmap to sustainable success, designed to help you build a thriving business while also living a fulfilling and balanced life. In conclusion, by following the roadmap laid out in this book, you will not only transition from operator to entrepreneur but also build a business that is ready for the future.

## *Case Study 1: Blockbuster versus Netflix – A Story of Failure and Success*

The Failure: Blockbuster was once the undisputed leader in the video rental industry. At its peak in the late 1990s, the company operated over 9,000 stores worldwide, with millions of customers renting movies and video games. Blockbuster's business model was built around physical storefronts where customers could browse and rent DVDs and VHS tapes. However, the company's leadership failed to recognize the fundamental shifts occurring in the industry and the broader market.

As technology advanced, streaming services and digital downloads began to emerge, offering customers more convenient ways to access entertainment without leaving their homes. Reed Hastings, the founder of Netflix, recognized this shift early on. Netflix initially started as a DVD rental service by mail, but Hastings understood that the future of entertainment consumption would be online. He began transitioning Netflix's business model from physical rentals to streaming content over the internet.

Blockbuster had the opportunity to adapt and even had

a chance to purchase Netflix for $50 million in 2000. However, the leadership at Blockbuster didn't understand the broader business they were in. They saw themselves as a retail chain, not as a company that delivered entertainment in the most convenient way possible. They continued to focus on their brick-and-mortar stores and failed to invest in digital technology.

The Consequence: Blockbuster's failure to understand and adapt to the evolving nature of its business led to its downfall. As Netflix grew rapidly by embracing streaming technology, Blockbuster's customer base dwindled. By the time Blockbuster attempted to launch its own streaming service, it was too late. The company filed for bankruptcy in 2010, and today, only one Blockbuster store remains as a relic of the past.

The Success: Netflix In contrast, Netflix's success is a testament to the importance of understanding the true nature of your business and being willing to evolve with the market. Reed Hastings recognized that the business wasn't just about renting DVDs – it was about providing customers with convenient, on-demand access to entertainment. By continuously adapting to technological advancements and consumer preferences, Netflix transformed itself into a global streaming giant, now producing its own content and boasting over 200 million subscribers worldwide.

Netflix's story illustrates how understanding the business you're truly in – beyond the products or services you offer – can lead to long-term success. It's about recognizing the broader value you provide to customers and being willing to evolve as the market changes.

### *Case Study 2: Kodak versus Fujifilm – A Tale of Divergent Paths*

The Failure: Kodak was once synonymous with photography. The company dominated the market for film and photographic equipment throughout most of the 20th century. Kodak's "Kodak Moment" tagline became part of popular culture, and the company was known for its high-quality film products. However, despite its success, Kodak failed to understand the broader business it was in.

In the 1970s, Kodak invented the first digital camera. However, fearing that digital photography would cannibalize its film business, Kodak's leadership chose not to pursue the technology. They believed that the core of their business was film, and they doubled down on their traditional products, investing heavily in maintaining their dominance in the film market.

As digital photography began to take off in the 1990s and 2000s, Kodak was slow to adapt. By the time they fully embraced digital technology, companies like Sony and Canon had already established themselves as leaders in the digital camera market. Kodak's failure to recognize that they were not in the "film" business but in the "imaging" business led to their decline.

The Consequence: Kodak's refusal to pivot and invest in digital technology resulted in the company filing for bankruptcy in 2012. While Kodak has since tried to reinvent itself in various ways, it never regained the market dominance it once had. The company's failure to understand the changing nature of the photography industry and its own business led to its downfall.

The Success: Fujifilm, a direct competitor to Kodak, faced the same challenges as digital photography began to replace film. However, Fujifilm's response was markedly different. The company's leadership understood that they were not just in the film business but in the broader business of imaging and chemistry. They recognized that the skills and technologies they had developed for film production could be applied to other industries.

Fujifilm invested heavily in research and development, expanding into new areas such as healthcare, cosmetics, and high-tech materials. For example, they applied their chemical expertise to create skincare products and developed digital imaging technologies for medical applications. Fujifilm also embraced digital photography early on, ensuring they remained relevant in the evolving market.

The Consequence: By understanding the broader business they were in and being willing to innovate and diversify, Fujifilm not only survived but thrived. Today, Fujifilm is a global conglomerate with a diversified portfolio, far removed from its origins as a film company. While Kodak struggled, Fujifilm successfully adapted and remains a profitable and influential company in multiple industries.

# CHAPTER 4:
# EMBRACING NEW TECHNOLOGIES

*"Any sufficiently advanced technology is indistinguishable from magic."*
— Arthur C. Clarke

To thrive in today's fast-paced business environment, entrepreneurs must harness the power of technology and make it a core part of their strategy. No longer is it enough to rely on tried-and-true methods; the most successful entrepreneurs are those who actively seek out and leverage the latest innovations to enhance their operations, improve customer experience, and gain a competitive edge. Technology has become the backbone of modern entrepreneurship, enabling businesses to scale, adapt, and thrive in ways that were unimaginable just a few decades ago.

To illustrate this point, let me introduce you to Stephen, a small business owner who was struggling to manage his growing company. Despite building a thriving business, Stephen found himself mired in operational tasks, leaving little time for strategic planning and visionary thinking. That all changed when Stephen's son Michael made the bold decision to embrace new technologies. By embracing cloud-based project management software and AI-powered marketing tools, they successfully automated routine tasks, freeing up valuable time and resources. This transformation allowed Stephen to focus on his true strengths: providing visionary leadership and driving innovation within the company.

Their story is a prime example of how entrepreneurs can shift their focus from operator to visionary by leveraging technology. In this chapter, we will explore the specific tools and innovations that are transforming the way entrepreneurs do business. From artificial intelligence and automation to customer relationship management (CRM) systems and data analytics, these technologies are not just "nice to have" but are essential for anyone looking to grow and scale a modern business.

## Why Now? The Technology Imperative for Modern Business

This chapter underscores the critical role that new technologies, particularly AI, play in modern business strategy. By embracing these advancements, entrepreneurs can drive efficiency, enhance customer experience, and make more informed decisions, all of which contribute to long-term success. The emphasis on continual investment in innovation and the strategic application of AI positions businesses to thrive in an increasingly competitive and technology-driven landscape.

The twenty-first century has witnessed an unprecedented rate of technological advancement, revolutionizing the way businesses operate and compete. From the rise of the internet to the proliferation of mobile devices, each wave of innovation has brought about profound changes in how businesses operate and compete. Today, we stand at the forefront of another significant shift – one driven by artificial intelligence (AI), machine learning, and automation. These technologies are not just tools for efficiency; they are transforming entire industries, creating new opportunities, and redefining the way businesses interact with customers and manage operations.

AI has moved from being a buzzword to becoming a critical component of modern business strategy. It has the potential to automate routine tasks, analyze vast amounts of data, and provide insights that were previously unimaginable. As an entrepreneur, your success hinges not on whether you'll adopt new technologies but on how strategically you implement them.

This technological revolution has far-reaching implications, transforming marketing, customer service, supply chain management, and product development processes. Companies that successfully embrace these advancements are better positioned to innovate, streamline their operations, and meet the evolving needs of their customers. On the other hand, those that resist or delay adoption risk falling behind in an increasingly competitive landscape.

The implications of this shift are vast. In the manufacturing sector, AI and automation are leading to the creation of "smart factories," where machines communicate with each other to optimize production processes. In finance, AI-driven algorithms are transforming trading, risk management, and customer service. In retail, AI is being used to personalize shopping experiences, manage inventory, and predict trends. The healthcare industry is leveraging AI for everything from diagnostics to personalized treatment plans.

To succeed in this new landscape, entrepreneurs must develop a deep understanding of these technologies and their potential applications within their specific industries. Embracing these advancements is not just about staying relevant; it's about gaining a competitive edge and positioning the business for future success.

## Investment in Innovation: Staying Ahead with New Technologies

In today's rapidly changing business environment, continual investment in innovation is essential for long-term success. The businesses that thrive are those that are not only willing to adopt new technologies but are also proactive in seeking out the latest advancements and integrating them into their operations. Investment in innovation is more than just a financial commitment; it's a mindset. It requires business leaders to prioritize research and development, encourage a culture of experimentation, and be willing to take calculated risks. This means setting aside resources – both time and money – for exploring new technologies, testing new ideas, and implementing solutions that can drive growth and efficiency. When my client Sarah initially resisted investing $10,000 in automation software, she was spending $50,000 annually on manual processes – a mindset shift that ultimately saved her business $40,000 yearly.

One of the key benefits of investing in innovation is that it allows businesses to stay ahead of the curve. By being early adopters of new technologies, companies can differentiate themselves from competitors, offer new and improved products or services, and enhance their operational efficiency. This proactive approach not only helps businesses remain competitive but also opens new revenue streams and market opportunities.

For entrepreneurs, the decision to invest in innovation should be guided by a clear understanding of the potential return on investment (ROI). This involves assessing how new technologies can improve various aspects of the business, from customer experience and product development to cost reduction and scalability. Although the initial costs of implementing new technologies may seem daunting, the long-term rewards – including enhanced efficiency, improved customer satisfaction, and expanded market share – typically far surpass the upfront investment.

Another critical aspect of investing in innovation is building the right partnerships. Collaborating with technology providers, startups, and research institutions can provide access to cutting-edge technologies and expertise that may not be available in-house. These partnerships can also help mitigate the risks associated with adopting new technologies by providing support and guidance throughout the implementation process.

For modern entrepreneurs, investing in innovation has become an absolute necessity rather than a choice. By continually seeking out and adopting new technologies, businesses can stay ahead of the competition, meet the changing needs of their customers, and drive long-term growth and profitability.

Here are some concrete examples of tools and platforms that can empower entrepreneurs and help business operators transition to a more visionary, strategic role. The following examples showcase practical applications of technology in areas such as productivity, automation, customer relationship management (CRM), and data analytics, demonstrating how entrepreneurs can leverage these tools to drive growth and improve efficiency.

## Examples of Technology Tools and Platforms

1. Automation and Workflow Tools
   - Zapier: Zapier is an automation tool that connects apps and services, allowing you to automate repetitive tasks. For example, Zapier can automatically save email attachments to cloud storage, create tasks in project management tools, or trigger notifications in communication platforms like Slack. This saves time, reduces manual work, and lets you focus on strategic tasks.
   - Automate.io: Similar to Zapier, Automate.io integrates with various applications, creating workflows that help streamline operations. It's great for businesses looking to automate sales, marketing, and customer support processes without requiring coding skills.
2. Customer Relationship Management (CRM) Systems
   - Salesforce: A powerful CRM platform, Salesforce helps manage customer data,

track interactions, and forecast sales. It's customizable and scalable, making it suitable for businesses of all sizes. Salesforce's AI feature, Einstein, offers predictive analytics to identify the best leads, enhancing your customer relationships and helping you make data-driven decisions.
- HubSpot: HubSpot's CRM is particularly useful for small and medium-sized businesses due to its ease of use and robust features. It includes marketing, sales, and service tools, all integrated to provide a seamless view of customer interactions. HubSpot's automation features can also nurture leads, manage email marketing, and help track sales metrics.

3. Data Analytics and Business Intelligence
   - Google Analytics: For businesses with an online presence, Google Analytics provides essential insights into website traffic, customer behavior, and conversion rates. It helps business owners make informed marketing and product decisions based on data trends, visitor demographics, and user activity.
   - Tableau: Tableau is a data visualization tool that translates complex data into clear, visual dashboards. It's ideal for companies looking to analyze large amounts of data, spot trends, and make informed strategic decisions. Tableau integrates with various data sources and can be used to track KPIs, sales figures, and customer insights.

4. Project Management and Collaboration
   - Asana: Asana is a project management platform designed to help teams organize tasks,

track deadlines, and communicate effectively. Business owners and team leaders can use Asana to assign responsibilities, monitor progress, and ensure that everyone is aligned with the company's goals and vision.
- Trello: Trello is a visual project management tool that's great for teams managing multiple projects or workflows. It uses boards, lists, and cards to break down tasks into manageable steps, making it ideal for overseeing daily operations, creative projects, or large-scale initiatives.

5. AI and Machine Learning Tools
    - Hootsuite: This social media management tool leverages AI to help businesses schedule posts, track engagement, and measure social media performance. Hootsuite's AI-driven insights can identify optimal posting times, track relevant conversations, and even suggest content ideas, saving time and boosting your digital presence.
    - X.AI: X.AI is an AI scheduling assistant that can handle meeting coordination autonomously. It integrates with calendar platforms like Google Calendar and Microsoft Outlook, helping business leaders streamline scheduling, which can be a major time drain.

6. Accounting and Financial Management
    - QuickBooks: QuickBooks is a leading accounting software that simplifies financial management by tracking expenses, invoicing clients, and generating financial reports. Its automated features, like receipt capture and tax calculation, are valuable for entrepreneurs who want to maintain financial accuracy without investing significant time in

accounting.
- FreshBooks: FreshBooks is another great tool for managing invoicing, time tracking, and expenses, particularly for small businesses and freelancers. FreshBooks' reporting features provide insights into cash flow and profitability, which can help in setting financial goals and making better spending decisions.

7. Communication and Remote Collaboration
    - Slack: Slack is a communication tool that allows for seamless remote communication within teams. With channels for specific topics and direct messaging, it's excellent for keeping project discussions organized. Slack also integrates with numerous other apps, allowing you to streamline notifications and reminders for the team.
    - Zoom: Zoom's video conferencing features are essential for remote collaboration, allowing you to hold team meetings, client presentations, and webinars. Its ease of use and scalability make it ideal for both small meetings and large events, bridging communication gaps in distributed teams.

8. Cybersecurity and Data Protection
    - Norton Small Business: Norton offers cybersecurity solutions designed for small businesses, providing tools to protect against malware, phishing, and ransomware. With data breaches becoming more common, investing in a robust security platform is essential for safeguarding sensitive business information.
    - LastPass: LastPass is a password management tool that securely stores passwords and

offers multi-factor authentication. It simplifies password management for business teams, reducing the risk of security breaches due to weak or reused passwords.

The above tools offer practical solutions for various operational needs, from automation and communication to financial management and cybersecurity.

## AI as a Tool: Leveraging AI for Efficiency, Customer Experience, and Decision-Making

Artificial Intelligence (AI) has emerged as one of the most powerful tools available to entrepreneurs today. Its applications are vast, and when leveraged effectively, AI can transform how businesses operate, interact with customers, and make decisions.

### *1. Improving Efficiency*

One of the most immediate benefits of AI is its ability to improve operational efficiency. AI-powered tools can automate routine tasks, freeing up employees to focus on higher-value activities. For example, AI-driven chatbots can handle customer inquiries, process transactions, and provide support around the clock, reducing the need for human intervention. In manufacturing, AI can optimize production schedules, predict maintenance needs, and reduce downtime, leading to significant cost savings.

AI can also enhance supply chain management by analyzing data to predict demand, optimize inventory levels, and identify potential disruptions before they occur. This level of automation and predictive analysis allows businesses to operate more efficiently, reduce waste, and improve overall productivity.

### *2. Enhancing Customer Experience*

AI is also revolutionizing the way businesses interact with their customers. Personalization, a key driver of customer satisfaction and loyalty, is made possible at scale through AI. By analyzing customer data, AI can deliver personalized recommendations, targeted marketing campaigns, and customized content that resonates with individual preferences.

For instance, e-commerce platforms use AI to recommend products based on a customer's browsing history, past purchases, and even their interactions with customer service. This level of personalization not only enhances the customer experience but also drives higher conversion rates and increases customer retention.

AI can also improve customer service by providing instant responses to inquiries and resolving issues more quickly. Advanced AI systems can analyze customer sentiment and adjust interactions in real-time to ensure a positive experience. This not only improves customer satisfaction but also reduces the workload on human customer service agents.

### *3. Data-Driven Decision-Making*

Perhaps one of the most transformative applications of AI is its ability to analyze vast amounts of data and provide actionable insights. In today's data-rich environment, businesses have access to more information than ever before. However, making sense of this data and using it to drive decisions can be challenging.

AI-powered analytics tools can process large datasets, identify patterns, and generate predictions that inform strategic decisions. For example, AI can analyze sales data to identify trends, forecast demand, and optimize pricing strategies. It can also be used to assess market conditions, competitor activity, and customer behavior, providing entrepreneurs with the insights they need to make informed decisions.

Harnessing the power of AI for data-driven decision-making empowers entrepreneurs to navigate uncertainty, mitigate risks, and seize opportunities with greater precision and confidence. This not only enhances the quality of decision-making but also enables businesses to respond more quickly to changes in the market.

This chapter underscores the critical role that new technologies, particularly AI, play in modern business strategy. By embracing these advancements, entrepreneurs can drive efficiency, enhance customer experience, and make more informed decisions, all of which contribute to long-term success. The emphasis on continual investment in innovation and the strategic application of AI positions businesses to thrive in an increasingly competitive and technology-driven landscape. To illustrate this, let's explore some relevant case studies where businesses have successfully leveraged AI and other technologies to gain a competitive edge.

## Case Study 1: Amazon – AI-Driven Customer Experience and Operational Efficiency

Background: Amazon, the e-commerce giant, is one of the most prominent examples of a company that has successfully integrated AI into its business model. From the very beginning, Amazon has been a technology-driven company, continuously innovating to improve its operations and customer experience.

AI Application: Amazon uses AI in several key areas:

1. Recommendation Engine: One of the most visible uses of AI at Amazon is its recommendation engine. By analyzing customer behavior, purchase history, and browsing patterns, Amazon's AI algorithms suggest products that customers are likely to be interested in. This personalization has been a significant factor in Amazon's ability to drive sales and increase customer engagement.

2. Supply Chain and Inventory Management: Amazon leverages AI to optimize its supply chain and inventory management. AI-powered systems predict demand for products, optimize inventory levels, and manage logistics to ensure that products are

delivered to customers as quickly and efficiently as possible. This has allowed Amazon to maintain its reputation for fast delivery and high customer satisfaction.
3. Alexa and Voice Commerce: Amazon's AI-powered voice assistant, Alexa, is another example of how the company uses technology to enhance the customer experience. Alexa enables customers to interact with Amazon's platform through voice commands, making it easier to search for products, place orders, and manage their shopping experience.

Impact: Amazon's strategic use of AI has played a crucial role in its dominance of the e-commerce industry. By continually investing in AI and other technologies, Amazon has been able to scale its operations, offer a personalized customer experience, and maintain its competitive edge in a highly dynamic market.

## Case Study 2: Netflix – AI in Content Personalization and Production

Background: Netflix, the leading streaming service, has built its success on a deep understanding of its customers and the strategic use of AI. As the company transitioned from DVD rentals to online streaming, it faced the challenge of retaining customers in an increasingly crowded market.

AI Application:

1. Content Personalization: Netflix's recommendation system is one of the most sophisticated AI applications in the entertainment industry. The platform uses AI to analyze viewers' watching habits, including what they watch, how long they watch, and even when they stop watching. This data is used to make personalized content recommendations, which have

been instrumental in keeping viewers engaged and reducing churn.
2. Content Production: AI also plays a role in Netflix's content production strategy. By analyzing viewing data, Netflix can identify trends and preferences that guide decisions about what content to produce or acquire. For example, the success of original series like "House of Cards" was driven by data insights that suggested a high demand for political dramas.

Impact: Netflix's use of AI has allowed it to not only personalize the viewing experience for its global audience but also to make data-driven decisions about content creation. This has helped Netflix maintain its position as a leader in the streaming industry, with a subscriber base that continues to grow.

## Case Study 3: Tesla – AI in Autonomous Driving and Manufacturing

Background: Tesla, the electric vehicle (EV) manufacturer, is at the forefront of using AI to revolutionize the automotive industry. Under the leadership of Elon Musk, Tesla has integrated AI into both its product offerings and its manufacturing processes.

AI Application:

- Autonomous Driving: Tesla's AI-driven Autopilot system is a key feature of its vehicles. Autopilot uses machine learning algorithms to process data from cameras, sensors, and radar to enable semi-autonomous driving. Tesla's Full Self-Driving (FSD) feature, currently in development, aims to achieve full autonomy, where the car can drive itself without human intervention.
- Manufacturing: AI is also heavily used in Tesla's manufacturing processes. The company's Gigafactories employ AI to optimize production lines,

reduce waste, and improve efficiency. AI-driven robots are used in the assembly of vehicles, ensuring high precision and quality control.

Impact: Tesla's investment in AI has positioned it as a leader in both the EV and autonomous driving markets. The company's ability to innovate with AI has not only set it apart from traditional automakers but has also driven significant advancements in the automotive industry.

## Case Study 4: Starbucks – AI in Customer Engagement and Operations

Background: Starbucks, the global coffeehouse chain, has successfully integrated AI into its operations to enhance customer experience and streamline its business processes. With thousands of locations worldwide, Starbucks needed a way to maintain consistency and engage customers on a personal level.

AI Application:

1. Personalized Marketing: Starbucks uses AI to power its personalized marketing efforts. The company's app collects data on customer preferences, order history, and location. This data is then used to deliver personalized offers and recommendations through the app, increasing customer loyalty and driving sales.
2. Inventory Management: AI helps Starbucks manage its supply chain and inventory across its global network of stores. By predicting demand for different products based on the time of day, season, and local events, AI ensures that stores are stocked appropriately, reducing waste and optimizing inventory levels.
3. Voice Ordering: Starbucks has also introduced voice-activated ordering through its app, which uses AI to understand and process customer orders. This feature enhances convenience and

improves the overall customer experience.

Impact: Starbucks' use of AI has enabled it to create a more personalized and efficient customer experience. By leveraging AI in both marketing and operations, Starbucks has maintained its competitive edge in the highly competitive coffeehouse market.

## Case Study 5: Walmart – AI in Retail Operations and Customer Service

Background: Walmart, the world's largest retailer, has embraced AI to stay competitive in the retail industry. As e-commerce giants like Amazon began to dominate, Walmart needed to innovate to maintain its position in the market.

AI Application:

1. Supply Chain Optimization: Walmart uses AI to optimize its vast supply chain. AI algorithms analyze data from across Walmart's network of suppliers, distribution centers, and stores to predict demand, optimize inventory levels, and reduce waste. This has helped Walmart improve efficiency and reduce costs in its operations.
2. Customer Service: Walmart has implemented AI-powered chatbots and virtual assistants to enhance customer service. These AI tools handle a range of customer inquiries, from tracking orders to answering product questions, freeing up human employees to focus on more complex tasks.
3. Store Operations: Walmart uses AI to monitor and manage store operations. For example, AI-powered cameras and sensors are used to monitor shelf inventory in real time, ensuring that popular products are always in stock. Additionally, AI-driven analytics help store managers make data-driven decisions about staffing and promotions.

Impact: Walmart's investment in AI has enabled it to

enhance its operational efficiency and customer service, allowing it to compete effectively in the retail industry. By leveraging AI, Walmart has successfully integrated technology into its traditional brick-and-mortar operations, positioning itself as a modern retail leader.

These case studies demonstrate the critical role that AI and other new technologies play in modern business strategy. Companies like Amazon, Netflix, Tesla, Starbucks, and Walmart have embraced AI not just as a tool but as a core component of their operations, driving efficiency, enhancing customer experience, and enabling data-driven decision-making. The success of these companies highlights the importance of continual investment in innovation and the strategic application of AI to thrive in an increasingly competitive and technology-driven landscape.

These case studies underscore the fact that thriving in today's competitive landscape demands more than a solid business plan; it necessitates an unwavering dedication to harnessing cutting-edge technologies to drive value creation, optimize operations, and provide unparalleled customer experiences. By following the lead of these industry giants, businesses of all sizes can harness the power of AI to achieve long-term success.

Avoiding the Pitfalls: Practical Steps for Entrepreneurs

1. Having guided numerous businesses through technological transformation, I have identified these key steps to ensure success:
2. Strategic Implementation: Begin with one core technology that directly addresses your biggest time drain. For example, if you're spending hours scheduling, start with an AI scheduling assistant.
3. Invest in Training: Technology is only as good as the people using it. Make sure you and your team are well-trained in the new systems.
4. Keep the Customer in Mind: Remember, the goal of technology is to enhance the customer

experience. Use data to better understand your customers' needs and tailor your strategies accordingly.
5. Monitor Results: Continuously assess the impact of the technology you implement. What works today might need tweaking tomorrow.

By following these steps, you can avoid common pitfalls and ensure that technology serves as a true asset in your entrepreneurial journey. Here are a few reflection questions to help you apply these lessons to your business.

## Reflection Questions

### *Technology Awareness*

- Are there specific areas in your business where technology could improve efficiency or performance?
- How familiar are you with the latest technologies in your industry?

### *Implementation Readiness*

- What barriers, if any, do you face in adopting new technologies?
- How can you start integrating small-scale tech solutions to prepare for a larger transformation?

### *AI and Automation Opportunities*

- Which repetitive tasks in your business could benefit from automation?
- How can you assess the ROI of new technology investments in your operations?

# CHAPTER 5: HARNESSING AI FOR BUSINESS GROWTH

*"I think it is possible for ordinary people to choose to be extraordinary."*
— Elon Musk

AI and automation have rapidly become game-changers for businesses across industries. Entrepreneurs who embrace these tools can streamline operations, reduce costs, and focus more on strategic growth. In this chapter, we will explore the seven key steps to successfully integrating AI and automation into your business, enabling you to stay competitive in a fast-changing world.

## Implementing AI and Automation: A Seven-Step Framework for Success

1. Identify the Areas of Your Business That Will Benefit Most: Begin by assessing your current operations and identifying areas where automation and AI can deliver the most significant benefits, such as customer service, marketing, or supply chain management.
2. Research the Right Tools for Your Needs: Not all AI tools are created equal. Spend time researching solutions that match your specific business requirements.

3. Set Clear Goals and Objectives: Establish clear objectives for your AI and automation initiatives, focusing on measurable outcomes such as time savings, error reduction, or sales growth.
4. Invest in Employee Training: Your team needs to be well-versed in these new technologies. Provide proper training and support to ensure a smooth transition.
5. Start Small and Scale Up: By starting small and scaling up, you can implement automation strategically, maximizing benefits while minimizing risks. This phased approach allows you to refine processes, manage costs, and build a strong foundation for long-term success.
6. Monitor and Adjust: Regularly track the performance of your automated systems. Be prepared to adjust as your business grows and technology evolves.
7. Evaluate ROI Continuously: Measure the return on investment for your AI and automation efforts, ensuring they deliver tangible results.

Now that we've outlined the steps, let me share a story that illustrates how these principles can translate into real-world success.

## Client Success Story: Transforming a Business with AI

Take Sarah, for example, the owner of a mid-sized retail company in Ecuador. Sarah was struggling to keep up with customer demands and manage her inventory efficiently. After identifying the potential for AI and automation, she implemented a customer service chatbot to handle routine inquiries and integrated an automated inventory management system.

Over the next few months, Sarah saw a dramatic increase in customer satisfaction and a significant reduction in lost sales due to stockouts. By following the seven steps outlined above, she was able to refocus her attention on growth strategies and product development, leaving the day-to-day tasks to the automation systems she had put in place.

## AI and Automation: Freeing Up Time for Strategic Thinking

In the modern business landscape, time is one of the most valuable resources. Entrepreneurs are often stretched thin, juggling a myriad of tasks that range from the strategic to the mundane. This is where Artificial Intelligence (AI) and automation come into play. By automating routine and repetitive tasks, AI can free up significant amounts of time, allowing business owners to focus on what truly matters: strategic thinking and long-term planning.

AI-powered automation can streamline a wide range of tasks, including data entry, scheduling, customer service, and inventory management, freeing up valuable time and resources. For example, AI-powered chatbots can manage customer inquiries 24/7, handling everything from basic questions to order processing. This not only reduces the workload on human employees but also ensures that customers receive prompt and consistent service.

In the realm of operations, AI can automate processes like invoice processing, payroll management, and supply chain logistics. By streamlining these tasks, businesses can reduce errors, improve efficiency, and lower operational costs. Moreover, automation allows for scalability, enabling businesses to grow without a corresponding increase in labor costs.

The real power of AI and automation lies in its ability to liberate business owners and their teams from routine tasks, allowing them to focus on strategic initiatives that drive growth and innovation. Instead of being bogged down by routine tasks, entrepreneurs can focus on high-level activities that drive growth, such as developing new products, exploring new markets, and refining their business strategies.

This shift from operational to strategic thinking is essential for any business looking to scale and achieve long-term success.

## AI for Decision Making: Enhancing Data Analysis, Market Predictions, and Customer Insights

One of the most powerful applications of AI in business is its ability to enhance decision-making through data analysis. In today's data-driven world, businesses generate and have access to vast amounts of information. However, sifting through this data and extracting actionable insights can be a daunting task. AI bridges this gap by providing powerful tools capable of analyzing vast datasets, uncovering hidden trends, and generating accurate predictions that surpass human capabilities alone.

Data Analysis: AI excels at processing and analyzing vast amounts of data quickly and accurately. Whether it's sales data, customer behavior, or operational metrics, AI can identify patterns and correlations that might go unnoticed by human analysts. These insights can inform everything from marketing strategies to product development, helping businesses make data-driven decisions that are more likely to succeed.

Market Predictions: Predictive analytics is another area where AI shines. By analyzing historical data and current market trends, AI can forecast future market conditions, helping businesses anticipate changes in demand, identify emerging opportunities, and mitigate potential risks. For instance, AI can predict sales trends based on seasonal patterns, economic indicators, and consumer sentiment, allowing businesses to adjust their strategies accordingly.

Customer Insights: Understanding customer behavior is crucial for any business looking to enhance customer satisfaction and loyalty. AI can analyze customer data to uncover insights into preferences, purchasing patterns, and pain points. This information can be used to personalize marketing efforts, optimize pricing strategies, and improve the overall customer experience. For example, AI can segment customers based on their behavior and preferences, enabling businesses to target them with personalized offers and communications.

By leveraging AI for decision-making, businesses can gain a deeper understanding of their operations, their market, and their customers. This not only improves the quality of decisions but also allows businesses to act more quickly and confidently in a rapidly changing environment.

## Implementing AI: A Step-by-Step Guide for Small and Medium-Sized Businesses

While integrating AI into a small or medium-sized business may appear challenging at first, a well-structured approach can make the process manageable and yield significant rewards. Here's a step-by-step guide to help you implement AI in your business:

### *Step 1: Identify the Opportunities*

The first step in implementing AI is to identify the areas of your business where AI can have the most significant impact. Begin by conducting a thorough evaluation of your existing operations, identifying tasks that are time-intensive, repetitive, or susceptible to errors. These are prime candidates for automation. Additionally, consider areas where better data analysis could lead to improved decision-making, such as customer insights, sales forecasting, or inventory management.

### *Step 2: Set Clear Objectives*

Once you've identified the opportunities for AI, set clear objectives for what you hope to achieve. Are you looking to improve efficiency, reduce costs, enhance customer service, or make more informed decisions? Establishing well-defined objectives will guide you in selecting the most appropriate AI tools and provide a framework for measuring their impact on your business.

## *Step 3: Choose the Right Tools*

There are many AI tools and platforms available, each designed to address specific business needs. When choosing AI solutions, consider factors such as ease of use, scalability, and integration with your existing systems. For small and medium-sized businesses, it's often best to start with AI tools that are user-friendly and don't require extensive technical expertise. Cloud-based AI solutions, for example, offer flexibility and can be scaled as your business grows.

## *Step 4: Start Small and Scale Gradually*

It's advisable to start with a pilot project to test the effectiveness of AI in your business. Choose a specific area where AI can deliver quick wins, such as automating customer inquiries or optimizing your inventory management. Once you've seen positive results, you can gradually expand AI to other areas of your business. This approach allows you to manage costs and minimize disruption while gaining confidence in your AI implementation.

A pilot project will allow you to assess the potential benefits and challenges of a new initiative on a smaller, manageable scale before committing fully. It typically involves implementing a new process, technology, or strategy on a small scale to test its effectiveness before a full rollout. Here's what it might entail:

- Defining Objectives and Scope: Set clear goals for the pilot, such as improving efficiency, reducing costs, or enhancing quality, and deciding on the specific area or process to test.
- Selecting Participants and Resources: Choose a small team or department to participate, ensuring they have the resources and training needed to implement the pilot effectively.
- Establishing Metrics for Success: Define key performance indicators (KPIs) that will measure the pilot's success, such as time savings, cost

reductions, or error rates, to assess impact.
- Testing and Monitoring: Run the pilot for a defined period, closely monitoring results, gathering feedback, and identifying any issues that arise.
- Analyzing Results and Making Adjustments: Evaluate the pilot's outcomes based on the metrics and feedback and make any necessary adjustments to improve the process.
- Preparing for Scaling: If the pilot is successful, use the insights gained to refine processes, provide additional training, and prepare for a full rollout across the organization.

### *Step 5: Train Your Team*

Successful AI implementation requires buy-in from your team. Invest in training to ensure that your employees understand how to use AI tools and are comfortable integrating them into their workflows. Emphasize the benefits of AI, such as reducing workload and freeing up time for more strategic tasks. A well-trained team will be more likely to embrace AI and use it effectively.

### *Step 6: Monitor and Optimize*

AI implementation is not a one-time project; it's an ongoing process. Continuously monitor the performance of your AI tools, evaluating their alignment with your predefined objectives and making data-driven adjustments as necessary. Collect feedback from your team and customers to identify areas for improvement. Be prepared to make adjustments and optimize your AI strategy as your business evolves and new technologies become available.

### *Step 7: Evaluate ROI*

Finally, evaluate the return on investment (ROI) of your AI implementation. When evaluating the ROI of your AI implementation, take into account both direct benefits, such as cost reductions and efficiency gains, and indirect advantages, including enhanced customer satisfaction and improved decision-making capabilities. By comparing the costs of AI implementation with the benefits achieved, you can determine the overall impact of AI on your business and make informed decisions about future investments.

This chapter provides a comprehensive guide for entrepreneurs looking to harness the power of AI to drive business growth. By automating routine tasks, enhancing decision-making, and following a structured approach to implementation, businesses can leverage AI to achieve greater efficiency, improve customer experience, and position themselves for long-term success.

Here's a basic cost-benefit framework for evaluating AI solutions, tailored to help you assess AI investments strategically and practically. Begin by precisely defining the specific challenge or opportunity that AI will tackle within your organization.

## Basic Cost-Benefit Framework for Evaluating AI Solutions

Implementing AI can transform a business, but it's essential to evaluate whether an AI solution will truly add value. This cost-benefit framework breaks down the key components to consider, helping you make an informed decision that aligns with your goals and resources.

## Step 1: Define Objectives and Scope

Start by clarifying the specific problem or opportunity AI will address in your business. Are you looking to automate tasks, improve customer service, enhance data analysis, or reduce operational costs? A well-defined scope will help you identify the most relevant AI solutions and measure their potential impact.

### *Questions to Ask*

- What business process or challenge are you aiming to improve with AI?

- How will success be measured? Define clear, measurable objectives such as cost savings, time reduction, or customer satisfaction improvements.

## Step 2: Estimate Costs

AI implementation costs can vary significantly, depending on the complexity of the solution and its integration needs. Consider the following categories of costs to get a clear picture of the investment required:

### 1. Direct Costs

- Software and Licensing: Costs for AI software and ongoing subscription fees.
- Implementation and Integration: Expenses for integrating the AI solution with existing systems.
- Training: Costs of training employees to use the AI solution effectively.
- Hardware: Include any necessary specialized hardware expenses, such as servers or GPUs, in your cost assessment for AI implementation.

### 2. Indirect Costs

- Maintenance and Support: Ongoing expenses for maintaining and updating the AI system.
- Potential Disruption: Temporary downtime or disruption to operations during implementation.
- Change Management: Time and resources needed to help employees adapt to new workflows or processes.

Total Estimated Costs = Direct Costs + Indirect Costs

## Step 3: Calculate Expected Benefits

Benefits of AI can be categorized into tangible (measurable) and intangible (non-measurable) outcomes. Here's how to evaluate each:

- Tangible Benefits

- Cost Savings: AI can reduce labor costs, save time, and increase productivity. Calculate potential savings by estimating time reductions or employee efficiency improvements.
- Revenue Growth: If the AI solution helps generate more sales (e.g., through targeted marketing or customer insights), estimate the potential revenue increase.
- Process Efficiency: AI can streamline processes, reducing errors and improving turnaround times. Quantify these savings where possible, such as by calculating reduced hours or fewer manual tasks.

- Intangible Benefits
  - Improved Customer Experience: AI can enhance customer satisfaction through faster response times, personalization, and proactive service. Although harder to quantify, these improvements often lead to higher retention rates and positive word-of-mouth.
  - Better Decision-Making: AI-driven analytics provide insights that improve decision-making. While intangible, the ability to make data-driven decisions can lead to long-term competitive advantages.
  - Scalability and Innovation: By embracing AI, your company can unlock new avenues for growth and innovation, establishing itself as a frontrunner in your industry.

Total Expected Benefits = Tangible + Intangible Benefits

## Step 4: Calculate ROI and Payback Period

To determine whether an AI solution is worth the investment, calculate the Return on Investment (ROI) and the Payback Period.

## ROI Calculation

If the ROI is positive and aligns with your financial goals, the AI solution may be a worthwhile investment.

Payback Period: The payback period is the time it will take to recoup the initial investment. Divide the Total Estimated Costs by the Annual Benefits (a subset of total benefits that occur annually):

A shorter payback period typically indicates a more attractive investment, as it means you'll see a return sooner.

## Step 5: Conduct a Risk Assessment

- Evaluate potential risks and consider creating contingency plans. AI solutions can sometimes underdeliver due to integration challenges, unforeseen expenses, or employee resistance. Identifying these risks early can help you address them effectively.
- Potential Risks to Consider:
- Data Privacy and Security: Implementing AI requires careful handling of data. Ensure that security and compliance measures are in place.
- Adoption Challenges: Employees may resist AI implementation if they feel it threatens their roles or requires a significant change in their work processes.
- Over-Reliance on Technology: Ensure there are backup systems and protocols in case of AI malfunction or downtime.

## Step 6: Make an Informed Decision

Leverage the insights derived from your comprehensive cost-benefit analysis and risk assessment to make an informed decision on whether to proceed with the AI implementation. If the expected benefits outweigh the costs and risks, and the ROI aligns with your business goals, the AI solution is likely a good fit. If not, consider either adjusting the project scope or exploring alternative solutions. Here's a breakdown of the cost-benefit analysis:

### *Category: Direct Costs*

- AI software license and implementation: Estimated cost of $20,000
- Training and integration: Estimated cost of $5,000

### *Category: Indirect Costs*

- Maintenance and support: Estimated cost of $2,500 annually
- Change management: Estimated cost of $1,500
- Total Estimated Costs: $29,000

### *Category: Tangible Benefits*

- Time saved on manual tasks: Estimated benefit of $15,000 annually
- Increased productivity: Estimated benefit of $10,000 annually

### *Category: Intangible Benefits*

- Improved customer experience: Hard to quantify
- Enhanced data-driven decision-making: Hard to quantify
- Total Expected Benefits: $25,000 annually + intangible benefits

ROI: 86 percent
Payback Period: 1.16 years

To demonstrate the real-world impact of AI in driving business growth and success, let's explore several case studies showcasing how companies across various industries have effectively leveraged AI to transform their operations.

## Case Study 1: Shopify – AI-Powered E-Commerce Solutions

Background: Shopify, a leading e-commerce platform,

enables entrepreneurs and businesses of all sizes to create and manage online stores. As e-commerce has grown, Shopify has continuously integrated AI into its platform to help its users better manage their businesses.

AI Application:

1. Automated Marketing: Shopify uses AI to power its marketing tools, allowing merchants to create and manage marketing campaigns more efficiently. AI-driven features include automated email marketing, customer segmentation, and personalized product recommendations. These tools help merchants reach the right customers with the right messages, driving higher conversion rates and sales.
2. Inventory Management: AI is also used in Shopify's inventory management system. By analyzing sales data and predicting demand, AI helps merchants optimize their inventory levels, reducing the risk of stockouts or overstocking. This leads to more efficient operations and improved profitability.
3. Customer Support: Shopify's AI-powered chatbots provide 24/7 customer support, helping merchants resolve common issues quickly. This not only enhances the customer experience but also frees up time for business owners to focus on more strategic tasks.

Impact: Shopify's integration of AI has enabled its users to automate routine tasks, improve their marketing efforts, and optimize inventory management. By leveraging AI, Shopify has helped small and medium-sized businesses scale more effectively, leading to increased growth and success for its customers.

## Case Study 2: H&M – AI in Fashion Retail

Background: H&M, the global fashion retailer, has turned to AI to improve various aspects of its operations, from inventory management to customer service. As the retail industry faces increasing pressure to innovate and adapt, H&M has embraced AI to stay competitive.

AI Application:

1. Demand Forecasting: H&M uses AI to forecast demand for its products. By analyzing historical sales data, weather patterns, and current fashion trends, AI helps H&M predict which products will be popular in specific locations. This allows the company to optimize its inventory and reduce waste, ensuring that the right products are available in the right stores at the right time.
2. Personalized Shopping Experience: H&M has also implemented AI-driven personalization in its online store. AI algorithms analyze customer behavior and preferences to offer personalized product recommendations, enhancing the shopping experience and increasing customer satisfaction.
3. Supply Chain Optimization: AI plays a crucial role in optimizing H&M's supply chain. By analyzing data from suppliers, manufacturing plants, and distribution centers, AI helps the company streamline its operations, reduce lead times, and minimize costs.

Impact: The use of AI has allowed H&M to improve its efficiency, reduce waste, and offer a more personalized shopping experience. These improvements have not only enhanced customer satisfaction but also contributed to the company's ability to grow and adapt in a highly competitive retail environment.

## Case Study 3: Coca-Cola – AI in Marketing and Product Development

Background: Coca-Cola, one of the world's most recognized brands, has leveraged AI to enhance its marketing strategies and product development processes. As the company continues to innovate, AI has become a critical tool for maintaining its market leadership.

AI Application:

1. Marketing Campaign Optimization: Coca-Cola uses AI to analyze vast amounts of consumer data, including social media activity, purchasing behavior, and market trends. This data is used to create highly targeted marketing campaigns that resonate with specific audiences. AI helps Coca-Cola optimize the timing, content, and delivery of these campaigns, resulting in higher engagement and better ROI.
2. Product Development: AI has also been used in Coca-Cola's product development process. By analyzing consumer preferences and feedback, AI helps the company identify potential new flavors and products that are likely to succeed in the market. For example, the development of Coca-Cola's Cherry Sprite flavor was guided by AI insights derived from social media data and customer feedback.
3. Supply Chain Efficiency: Coca-Cola has implemented AI to optimize its supply chain operations. AI-driven analytics help the company predict demand, manage inventory, and optimize distribution routes, ensuring that products are delivered efficiently and cost-effectively.

Impact: Coca-Cola's use of AI has enabled the company to enhance its marketing efforts, streamline product development, and improve supply chain efficiency. By leveraging AI, Coca-Cola has maintained its competitive edge and continued to grow its global presence.

## Case Study 4: Alibaba – AI in E-commerce and Logistics

Background: Alibaba, one of the largest e-commerce companies in the world, has made significant investments in

AI to improve its platform and logistics operations. AI plays a central role in Alibaba's ability to handle millions of transactions daily and deliver a seamless shopping experience.

AI Application:

1. Product Recommendations: Alibaba's e-commerce platforms, including Taobao and Tmall, use AI to analyze customer behavior and preferences. This data is used to generate personalized product recommendations, increasing the likelihood of purchase and enhancing the overall shopping experience.
2. Chatbots and Customer Service: Alibaba has deployed AI-powered chatbots to handle customer inquiries and provide support. These chatbots can process millions of queries simultaneously, offering instant assistance to shoppers and reducing the burden on human customer service representatives.
3. Logistics and Delivery: AI is integral to Alibaba's logistics network, Cainiao. AI-driven systems optimize delivery routes, predict package arrival times, and manage warehouse operations. This ensures that products are delivered quickly and efficiently, even during peak shopping periods like Singles' Day.

Impact: Alibaba's strategic use of AI has allowed it to scale its operations and offer a superior customer experience. By automating routine tasks and optimizing logistics, Alibaba has maintained its position as a global e-commerce leader while continuing to grow its business.

## Case Study 5: American Express – AI in Financial Services

Background: American Express (Amex), a leading financial services company, has embraced AI to enhance its offerings and improve customer service. In the highly competitive financial services industry, AI has become a key differentiator for Amex.

AI Application:

1. Fraud Detection: Amex uses AI to detect and prevent fraudulent transactions. AI algorithms analyze transaction patterns in real-time, identifying anomalies that may indicate fraud. This allows Amex to take immediate action to protect its customers and reduce financial losses.
2. Customer Experience: Amex has integrated AI into its customer service operations. AI-powered chatbots handle routine inquiries, such as account balances and payment due dates, while human agents focus on more complex issues. This approach enhances customer satisfaction by providing quick and efficient service.
3. Personalized Offers: AI is also used to analyze customer spending habits and preferences. This data is leveraged to create personalized offers and rewards, tailored to each customer's unique needs and interests. These targeted offers drive customer loyalty and increase engagement.

Impact: The implementation of AI has enabled American Express to enhance fraud detection, improve customer service, and offer personalized experiences. These advancements have strengthened Amex's brand reputation and contributed to its continued growth in the financial services industry.

## The Strategic Use of AI for Business Growth

These case studies demonstrate the practical application of AI in driving business growth across various industries. Companies like Shopify, H&M, Coca-Cola, Alibaba, and American Express have successfully harnessed AI to automate routine tasks, enhance decision-making, and improve customer experience. By integrating AI into their operations, these businesses have achieved greater efficiency, scalability, and long-term success.

For entrepreneurs, these examples highlight the potential of AI to transform small and medium-sized businesses. By following a structured approach to AI implementation, companies can realize the benefits quickly and position themselves for sustained growth in an increasingly competitive and technology-driven landscape.

Here are some reflection questions to help you apply the scaling through AI and automation lessons to your businesses.

## AI in Operations

- Are you currently using any AI tools in your business? If not, what's holding you back?
- How might AI streamline one area of your business?

## Evaluating Automation Benefits

- Which processes would benefit most from automation, and how would this impact your team's productivity?
- What potential outcomes (e.g., time savings, cost reductions) could come from automation?

## Leadership and AI Integration

- What is your role in guiding AI adoption within your business?
- How can you ensure AI and automation align with your business goals and company culture?

# CHAPTER 6:
# MOVING BEYOND OPERATIONS

*"The only way to discover the limits of the possible is to go beyond them into the impossible."*
*– Arthur C. Clarke*

While every entrepreneur begins by wearing multiple hats, there comes a crucial point in the growth journey when relinquishing operational control becomes necessary to achieve the next level of success. Moving beyond operations doesn't mean disregarding the details; it means trusting others to handle them so that you can guide the overall vision. As you evolve into a true leader, your role shifts from task management to creating an environment where others can excel. This chapter provides the tools to make that leap, helping you identify practical steps and transition exercises that encourage a new approach to leadership.

By delegating tasks, building a strong team, and embracing your role as a visionary leader, you can position your business for long-term success. To unlock your business's full potential, you must elevate your focus from managing daily operations to defining your company's strategic direction, fostering a culture of innovation, and inspiring your team to bring your collective vision to life.

## Why Moving Beyond Operations is Crucial for Entrepreneurial Success

In the early stages of a business, it's natural for

entrepreneurs to be deeply involved in daily operations. Whether it's managing client relationships, overseeing product development, or handling the company's finances, many founders wear multiple hats to ensure the business runs smoothly. However, there comes a point in every successful business journey when the focus needs to shift from being an operator to becoming a true entrepreneur and leader. This shift is not just beneficial – it's essential for long-term growth and sustainability.

Remaining mired in the daily operational grind can severely restrict your ability to envision and pursue the full potential of your business. An excessive focus on tactical tasks can obscure your view of the broader strategic landscape, causing you to miss valuable opportunities for growth and innovation. You might miss out on strategic opportunities or fail to anticipate shifts in the market that could make or break your business. Entrepreneurs who successfully transition out of operational roles gain the freedom to think more creatively, develop long-term strategies, and guide their companies toward innovation and growth.

One of the key reasons why this shift is so crucial is scalability. As your business grows, the operational demands will only increase. As an entrepreneur, your personal involvement in the company's operational minutiae directly limits your capacity to scale, as your time and energy become the primary bottlenecks to growth. At this stage, delegation and systemization become vital. By stepping back from operations and empowering your team to handle those tasks, you can devote more time to activities that drive growth – such as expanding your market reach, building strategic partnerships, and innovating your product or service offerings.

Moreover, shifting your focus from operations to strategy allows you to develop a stronger leadership role. By stepping back from micromanagement, you can dedicate your attention to nurturing talent, fostering a culture of innovation, and creating an environment where your team can thrive. Leadership is not just about managing; it's about inspiring your team to execute your vision while you steer the business toward new horizons. Without this shift, you may find it challenging to attract and retain top talent who are looking for a dynamic, forward-thinking company.

Another crucial reason for this shift is to future-proof your business. The business landscape is constantly changing, with new technologies, market trends, and consumer behaviors emerging all the time. Entrepreneurs who are consumed by daily operational demands frequently find themselves in a reactive mode, struggling to keep pace with change rather than proactively shaping the future of their business. By transitioning to a more entrepreneurial role, you can keep your finger on the pulse of industry trends, explore new opportunities, and ensure your business remains adaptable in a fast-changing environment.

Finally, moving beyond operations is essential for personal growth and sustainability as an entrepreneur. Burnout is a real risk when you are too immersed in every aspect of the business. Taking a step back allows you to focus on what truly matters – both for the business and for your well-being. Entrepreneurs who successfully make this transition often find renewed passion for their work and a greater sense of purpose in their leadership roles.

In summary, shifting your focus from operations to entrepreneurship is not just about improving the efficiency of your business; it's about unlocking its full potential. By letting go of the day-to-day tasks, you can guide your company to new heights and ensure it remains competitive, innovative, and scalable in the long run. The following sections will outline the practical steps to help you make this critical transition.

## Delegate to Elevate: The Power of Letting Go

As an entrepreneur, it's natural to want to be involved in every aspect of your business. After all, it's your vision, your hard work, and your passion that have brought it to life.

However, one of the most critical steps in growing your business is learning to delegate operational tasks. Delegation is not about relinquishing control; it's about empowering your team to take ownership of their roles, which in turn allows you to focus on what truly drives growth – strategic planning, innovation, and leadership.

When entrepreneurs get bogged down in daily operations, they risk losing sight of the bigger picture. The time spent managing routine tasks is time taken away from activities that could propel the business forward. By delegating, you free up valuable time and mental space to think strategically about your business's future.

Delegation starts with identifying which tasks can be handled by others. These might include administrative duties, customer service, logistics, or even certain aspects of sales and marketing. Once you've identified these tasks, the next step is to delegate them to capable team members or hire additional staff if needed.

Effective delegation is not merely a means of offloading tasks; it is an essential tool for empowering your team, fostering trust, and enabling them to develop the decision-making skills necessary for your business to thrive and grow. This trust is crucial for fostering a sense of ownership and accountability among your employees. When team members feel empowered, they are more likely to take the initiative, solve problems, and contribute to the business's success.

Delegating also involves clear communication and setting expectations. Provide your team with the resources, training, and guidance they need to succeed, but resist the urge to micromanage. Instead, focus on the outcomes and give your team the freedom to determine how to achieve them.

By delegating operational tasks, you elevate your role from manager to leader, allowing you to concentrate on high-level activities that align with your long-term vision for the business.

## Building a Strong Team: The Foundation of Operational Excellence

The success of your delegation efforts hinges on the strength of your team. Building a capable and reliable team is essential for ensuring that daily operations run smoothly, even when you're not involved in the day-to-day details.

Hiring the Right People: The first step in building a strong team is hiring the right people. Look for individuals who not only have the necessary skills and experience but also share your company's values and vision. Prioritizing cultural fit is essential, as team members who embrace your company's mission and values are more likely to demonstrate higher levels of engagement, motivation, and dedication to driving the business forward. Employees who are aligned with your business's mission are more likely to be engaged, motivated, and committed to the company's success.

During the hiring process, consider candidates' problem-solving abilities, adaptability, and willingness to learn. In a rapidly changing business environment, these traits are often more valuable than specific technical skills, which can be taught. Seek out individuals who demonstrate initiative and a strong work ethic, as they are likely to thrive in a dynamic and growing business.

Training and Development: Once you've assembled your team, investing in their ongoing training and development is key to maintaining operational excellence. Provide opportunities for skill development, whether through formal training programs, workshops, or on-the-job learning. Encourage a culture of continuous improvement, where employees are empowered to seek out new knowledge and apply it to their roles.

Regular feedback and performance reviews are also essential for helping your team grow. Constructive feedback helps employees understand their strengths and areas for improvement, while recognition of their achievements boosts morale and motivation.

Empowering Your Team: True empowerment extends beyond mere delegation; it necessitates the creation of a workplace culture in which team members feel genuinely valued, trusted, and confident in their ability to make impactful decisions. Encourage open communication and collaboration and provide your team with the tools and resources they need to excel in their roles.

One way to empower your team is to involve them in decision-making processes. When employees have a say in how the business is run, they are more likely to be invested in its success. This can lead to increased innovation, improved problem-solving, and a stronger sense of ownership.

A strong team not only handles daily operations efficiently but also contributes to the strategic growth of the business. When your team is capable, motivated, and aligned with your vision, you can confidently delegate tasks and focus on leading the company to new heights.

## Visionary Leadership: Setting the Direction for Your Company

As an entrepreneur, your most important role is that of a visionary leader. While your team manages the operations, your focus should be on setting the direction for the company and driving it toward its long-term goals.

At its core, visionary leadership involves crafting a vivid and inspiring vision for your business's future that resonates with your team and stakeholders alike. This vision should inspire and motivate your team, guiding their efforts and decisions. It's your responsibility to articulate this vision and ensure that every aspect of the business aligns with it.

Being a visionary leader also means staying ahead of industry trends and anticipating changes in the market. It requires you to be forward-thinking, always looking for new opportunities to innovate, grow, and expand your business. This proactive approach is what sets successful entrepreneurs apart from those who merely react to changes as they occur.

To be an effective visionary leader, you must also be adaptable. The business landscape is constantly evolving, and your vision may need to evolve with it. This doesn't mean abandoning your core values or mission but rather being open to new ideas, technologies, and strategies that can help you achieve your goals.

Rather than claiming to have all the answers, visionary leaders distinguish themselves by asking thought-provoking questions, embracing curiosity, and fostering an environment that encourages the exploration of innovative ideas and untapped opportunities. It's about creating a culture of innovation where your team feels empowered to contribute ideas and take risks in pursuit of the company's vision.

As a visionary leader, your role is to guide your business toward a future that is both ambitious and achievable. This requires a combination of strategic thinking, creativity, and the ability to inspire and lead others. By dedicating your attention to strategic planning, market analysis, and fostering key partnerships while entrusting operational responsibilities to your skilled team, you can chart a course for your business that leads to lasting growth and success.

This chapter emphasizes the importance of moving beyond operations to focus on strategic growth and visionary leadership. By delegating tasks, building a strong team, and embracing your role as a visionary leader, you can position your business for long-term success. The key is to elevate your thinking from managing daily operations to setting the direction for your company and inspiring your team to achieve your shared vision.

## Practical Transition Exercises for Shifting from Operator to Leader Mindset

To support your transition from an operational to a strategic and visionary mindset, engage in the following exercises designed to gradually shift your focus and build the habits necessary for effective leadership.

### *1. Daily Vision Review*

- This exercise helps keep the big picture top of mind, pushing you to start each day from a leader's perspective.
- Action: Each morning, take ten minutes to review your business's long-term goals and strategic vision. Identify three actions you can take during the day to move closer to these goals, even if they're small.
- Purpose: Over time, this practice strengthens your ability to prioritize strategic decisions and resist getting bogged down in operational tasks.

## 2. Task Delegation Audit

This exercise assists in identifying tasks that can be delegated, allowing you to focus more on strategic responsibilities.

- Action: List all tasks you handle in a typical week. Separate them into two categories: Strategic and Operational. For each operational task, identify team members who could take on these responsibilities with proper training or support.
- Purpose: Delegation can feel challenging, but this audit provides a clear pathway for transferring routine tasks, freeing up your time to focus on high-level strategy.

## 3. Weekly Strategy Time Block

Setting aside dedicated time for strategy is crucial for cultivating a leader mindset.

- Action: Block two to three hours weekly for strategic thinking, planning, and research. Use this time to work on high-level projects, assess industry trends, or brainstorm future opportunities.
- Purpose: Protecting this time reinforces the value of strategic work and helps you break the cycle of reactionary tasks. Over time, this habit shifts your

mindset from daily operations to long-term planning.

## 4. Future-Oriented Decision-Making

To develop the entrepreneurial perspective, practice evaluating decisions based on long-term impact rather than short-term gains.

- Action: For each major decision, ask, "How does this align with our long-term goals?" Consider creating a pros-and-cons list that weighs both immediate and future impacts.
- Purpose: This exercise trains you to adopt a future-focused outlook, an essential skill for leaders aiming to build a sustainable business.

Here are some case studies that illustrate successful business practices where leaders moved beyond operations to drive strategic growth.

## Case Study 1: Howard Schultz and Starbucks – From Operations to Global Strategy

Background: Howard Schultz joined Starbucks in 1982 as Director of Retail Operations and Marketing. At the time, Starbucks was a small coffee retailer in Seattle with just a few stores. Schultz had a vision to transform Starbucks from a small regional player into a global brand known for its coffee culture.

Moving Beyond Operations: Recognizing that his vision for Starbucks required a shift in focus, Schultz made the crucial decision to distance himself from daily operational concerns and concentrate his efforts on strategic initiatives that would drive the company's long-term growth. He began by delegating operational tasks to capable managers, freeing up his time to focus on expanding the brand and developing a strategic plan for growth.

Schultz's leadership approach emphasized creating a unique customer experience, building a strong company culture, and expanding globally. He focused on developing a brand that was not just about selling coffee but about creating a "third place" between home and work where people could relax, socialize, and enjoy high-quality beverages.

Impact: Under Schultz's visionary leadership, Starbucks grew from a small local chain to a global powerhouse with thousands of stores worldwide. By moving beyond operations and focusing on strategy, Schultz was able to position Starbucks as a global brand that continues to thrive today.

## Case Study 2: Steve Jobs and Apple – Embracing Visionary Leadership

Background: Steve Jobs co-founded Apple in 1976, and he was deeply involved in the development of the company's early products, such as the Apple I and Apple II computers. However, by the mid-1980s, internal conflicts led to Jobs leaving the company. During his absence, Apple struggled with its identity and market position.

Moving Beyond Operations: When Jobs returned to Apple in 1997, the company was on the brink of bankruptcy. Recognizing that he needed to move beyond day-to-day operations, Jobs focused on revitalizing Apple's brand and product strategy. He delegated operational responsibilities to trusted executives, allowing him to concentrate on innovation and long-term vision.

By prioritizing innovation and strategic thinking over operational management, Jobs' visionary leadership paved the way for the creation of revolutionary products like the iMac, iPod, iPhone, and iPad, which redefined entire industries and solidified Apple's position as a global technology leader. He emphasized design, user experience, and the integration of hardware and software, setting Apple apart from its competitors.

Impact: Jobs' ability to move beyond operations and embrace his role as a visionary leader transformed Apple into one of the most valuable companies in the world. His focus on strategic growth and innovation redefined entire industries, and Apple's products continue to influence technology and culture globally.

## Case Study 3: Jeff Bezos and Amazon – From Online Bookstore to Global Conglomerate

Background: Jeff Bezos founded Amazon in 1994 as an online bookstore. In its early years, Bezos was heavily involved in the day-to-day operations of the business, from managing inventory to handling customer service. However, as Amazon grew, Bezos recognized the need to transition from an operational role to a strategic one.

Moving Beyond Operations: Bezos delegated operational tasks to a skilled management team and began focusing on Amazon's long-term strategy. He envisioned Amazon as "the everything store," where customers could find and buy anything they needed online. This vision led to the expansion of Amazon's product offerings, the development of Amazon Web Services (AWS), and the introduction of innovations like Prime and Kindle.

As a strategic leader, Bezos prioritized an unwavering focus on customer needs, a relentless pursuit of innovation, and a bold approach to experimentation and risk-taking, which became the guiding principles behind Amazon's rapid growth and diversification. He focused on long-term growth rather than short-term profits, allowing Amazon to dominate multiple markets, including e-commerce, cloud computing, and digital entertainment.

Impact: By moving beyond operations and focusing on strategic growth, Bezos transformed Amazon from a small online bookstore into one of the most influential companies in the world. Amazon's success is a testament to the power of visionary leadership and the importance of delegating operational tasks to focus on the bigger picture.

## Case Study 4: Indra Nooyi and PepsiCo – Strategic Transformation and Growth

Background: Indra Nooyi joined PepsiCo in 1994 and

quickly rose through the ranks to become CEO in 2006. At the time, PepsiCo was known primarily for its snack foods and sugary beverages, but Nooyi recognized that consumer preferences were shifting toward healthier options.

Moving Beyond Operations: As CEO, Nooyi moved beyond the operational aspects of the business to focus on strategic growth and transformation. She launched the "Performance with Purpose" initiative, which aimed to align PepsiCo's business goals with sustainability and health. Nooyi pushed for the development of healthier products, expanded the company's global footprint, and invested in research and development to innovate new offerings.

Nooyi also focused on building a strong leadership team, delegating day-to-day operations to her executives while she concentrated on long-term strategy. Her leadership style emphasized collaboration, diversity, and inclusion, helping to foster a strong company culture.

Impact: Under Nooyi's leadership, PepsiCo experienced significant growth and diversification, expanding its product portfolio to include healthier options and sustainable practices. Her focus on strategic transformation ensured that PepsiCo remained competitive in a rapidly changing market. Nooyi's ability to move beyond operations and embrace visionary leadership positioned PepsiCo for continued success in the future.

## Case Study 5: Sheryl Sandberg and Facebook – Scaling Operations and Strategic Growth

Background: Sheryl Sandberg joined Facebook as COO in 2008, when the company was still a relatively small startup. At the time, Facebook's operations were not yet scalable, and the company needed to develop a sustainable business model.

Moving Beyond Operations: Sandberg's role at Facebook was to scale the company's operations and develop a long-term strategy for growth. She focused on building a robust advertising platform that would drive revenue while also expanding Facebook's global user base. Sandberg delegated many operational tasks to her team, allowing her to focus on strategic initiatives such as expanding into international markets and developing partnerships.

In addition to her strategic initiatives, Sandberg recognized the importance of cultivating a robust company culture and championing diversity and inclusion as essential components of Facebook's long-term success, demonstrating her understanding that effective leadership extends beyond operational concerns. She emphasized the importance of empowering employees and creating an environment where innovation could thrive.

Impact: Sandberg's strategic leadership helped transform Facebook from a startup into a global tech giant. By moving beyond operations and focusing on strategic growth, Sandberg played a crucial role in Facebook's success, including its ability to generate significant revenue through advertising and expand its influence across the globe.

## The Power of Visionary Leadership

These case studies highlight the importance of moving beyond operations to focus on strategic growth and visionary leadership. Leaders like Howard Schultz, Steve Jobs, Jeff Bezos, Indra Nooyi, and Sheryl Sandberg demonstrate that delegating operational tasks and concentrating on long-term strategy can drive significant business growth and success. By embracing their roles as visionary leaders, these individuals were able to guide their companies to new heights, inspiring their teams to achieve shared goals and positioning their businesses for sustained success in an ever-changing market.

For entrepreneurs, these examples serve as a powerful reminder that true leadership involves stepping back from daily operations and looking at the bigger picture. By focusing on strategic growth and inspiring your team, you can create a thriving business that continues to evolve and succeed in the long term.

Here are reflection questions to help you apply the lessons of shifting from Operator to Entrepreneur to your business.

## Reflection Questions

### *Evaluating Your Role*

- What parts of your current role are operator-focused versus entrepreneur-focused?
- How can you begin to transfer more responsibilities to others?

### *Long-Term Vision and Strategy*

- What unique strengths do you bring to your business as a visionary leader?
- How can you redefine your role to make the most of these strengths?

### *Measuring Success in Your New Role*

- What metrics will help you assess the success of your shift from operator to entrepreneur?
- How can you track progress on both personal and business levels?

## CHAPTER 7:
## SCALING FOR SUCCESS

*"Whether you think you can, or you think you can't – you're right."*
– Henry Ford

Scaling is a critical component of ensuring long-term business sustainability and profitability. More than simply boosting sales, scaling involves constructing a robust model capable of accommodating increased demand while maintaining the highest standards of quality, efficiency, and customer satisfaction.

Achieving growth demands a shift in mindset from working in the business to working on the business. By investing in scalable systems, processes, and technology, you establish a solid foundation for sustainable expansion. This section covers essential principles of scalability, guiding you in recognizing when your business is ready to grow and ensuring that growth remains both manageable and enduring.

Building sustainable growth isn't just about expanding quickly; it's about creating a foundation that supports long-term success while preserving the quality and values that define your business. When approached strategically, growth allows you to reach more customers, broaden your offerings, and boost revenue – all while maintaining operational efficiency. This chapter guides you through the essential steps for effective growth and offers practical metrics to track progress, empowering you to expand confidently without losing control.

## Key Metrics and KPIs for Tracking Scaling Progress

Tracking specific metrics and key performance indicators (KPIs) is vital for ensuring your business scales effectively. These KPIs will provide clear benchmarks and help you identify areas for improvement as your business grows. Here are some essential metrics to consider, which you can offer as a downloadable resource or bonus for readers who reach out to you:

### *Revenue Growth Rate*

This metric measures the percentage increase in revenue over a specified period. A healthy revenue growth rate is a strong indicator that your business can handle increased demand without significant issues.

### *Customer Acquisition Cost (CAC)*

CAC helps you understand how much you're spending to acquire each new customer. As you scale, your goal should be to lower CAC by increasing efficiency in your marketing and sales efforts.

### *Customer Lifetime Value (CLV)*

CLV indicates the total revenue you can expect from a single customer over their lifetime. As you scale, a higher CLV signals that you're retaining customers longer and increasing their spending, which boosts profitability.

### *Gross Profit Margin*

This metric serves as a key indicator of your business's efficiency in producing goods or services. Sustaining or enhancing your gross profit margin throughout the scaling process demonstrates that your growth strategy is not sacrificing profitability.

### *Operational Efficiency Ratio*

This ratio shows how well you're managing operational costs relative to revenue. As you scale, lowering this ratio means you're achieving growth with minimal increases in operating expenses, a key indicator of efficient scaling.

### *Employee Productivity (Revenue per Employee)*

Revenue per employee indicates productivity and efficiency within your team. As you grow, this metric should ideally increase, signaling that your team structure supports expansion without needing a proportional increase in staff.

### *Customer Retention Rate*

This rate reflects your ability to keep customers over time, which is crucial for sustainable scaling. A high retention rate is typically a good sign that your business model and customer experience are resilient.

### *Churn Rate*

Monitoring churn rate helps identify how many customers you're losing over time. Reducing churn is essential for scaling because it's often more cost-effective to retain existing customers than to acquire new ones.

### *Net Promoter Score (NPS)*

As a measure of customer satisfaction and loyalty, NPS provides valuable insights into the likelihood of customers recommending your business to others. Achieving high NPS scores during scaling suggests that your growth is supported by a strong foundation of customer advocacy, fueling organic, word-of-mouth expansion.

### *Inventory Turnover Ratio (for product-based businesses)*

This ratio measures how often inventory is sold and replaced within a period. High turnover rates suggest efficient inventory management, which is vital for scaling product-based businesses without surplus costs.

## Leveraging Metrics to Scale with Confidence

By tracking these metrics and KPIs, you can keep a pulse on your scaling progress and adjust as needed. Recognizing that scaling is not a uniform, one-size-fits-all endeavor is crucial. To ensure that your growth trajectory remains in harmony with your financial objectives, team capabilities, and overarching vision, a process of continuous evaluation and adjustment is necessary. These metrics will serve as guiding indicators, allowing you to scale in a way that's sustainable, profitable, and aligned with the entrepreneurial mindset.

This chapter guides entrepreneurs through the process of scaling their businesses by transitioning from operator to CEO, creating strategic plans that align with their vision, and tracking the key metrics that drive growth. By focusing on leadership, strategic planning, and data-driven decision-making, entrepreneurs can position their businesses for sustainable success and continued expansion.

## The Importance of Scaling for Long-Term Success

Scaling is one of the most critical phases of a business's lifecycle. Although launching a business calls for passion, creativity, and resilience, the process of scaling a business necessitates a distinct set of competencies and strategic approaches. Scaling is about moving beyond "survival mode" and positioning your business for sustainable, long-term growth. "Survival mode" for a business typically involves a focus on immediate, day-to-day needs at the expense of long-term planning or growth. Here's a brief example: A small retail business is struggling with cash flow due to fluctuating sales and rising operational costs. To keep the doors open, the owner spends every day managing urgent tasks: cutting expenses wherever possible, negotiating with vendors for delayed payments, and offering heavy discounts to boost short-term sales. Employees are overworked, morale is low, and the owner lacks the time or resources to invest in marketing, training, or technology upgrades. The business can only think as far as the next payroll or rent payment, making it nearly impossible to plan for growth or explore new opportunities. In this "survival mode," the business is focused on staying afloat from one month to the next, leaving little room for strategy or innovation that could lead to sustainable success.

Scaling involves expanding your operations, increasing your capacity to meet demand, and maximizing your impact in the marketplace. Without a clear strategy for scaling, even the most promising businesses can plateau or, worse, falter in the face of growing competition.

The benefits of scaling go far beyond increasing revenue. When done strategically, scaling allows your business to capitalize on economies of scale, reducing the cost per unit as production or service delivery expands. This efficiency gives your business a competitive edge by allowing you to offer more value to your customers without significantly increasing your operational costs. In turn, this can boost profitability, giving you the resources to reinvest in the business, attract top talent, and fuel innovation.

In addition to improving efficiency, scaling is necessary for staying competitive. In today's fast-paced business environment, companies that don't grow are quickly left behind. Competitors are always looking for ways to increase their market share, and consumer expectations are constantly evolving. Scaling allows you to meet these challenges head-on by expanding your product or service offerings, reaching new markets, and continuously improving your value proposition. Effective scaling enables your business to not merely match the pace of your competitors but also to distinguish itself as a trailblazer and innovator within your industry.

Another key benefit of scaling is increased brand recognition and market presence. As your business grows, so does its visibility, allowing you to attract more customers and forge stronger relationships with partners, investors, and other stakeholders. A scaled business has the potential to become a household name, expanding its influence and solidifying its reputation in the market. This heightened brand recognition can also create new opportunities for collaboration, licensing, and partnerships that were previously out of reach.

Moreover, scaling plays a pivotal role in fortifying your business's resilience. By diversifying revenue streams, expanding your customer base, and creating a more adaptable organizational structure, scaling helps insulate your business from the risks associated with overreliance on a single product, market, or client. A company that remains small and is overly dependent on a limited customer base or narrow product offering is vulnerable to market shifts, economic downturns, and changes in consumer behavior. By scaling, you can diversify your revenue streams and reduce your dependence on any one aspect of the business. This diversification makes your company more adaptable and better positioned to weather challenges and seize opportunities in changing economic conditions.

Lastly, scaling is essential for personal and professional growth. As an entrepreneur, leading a scalable business allows you to step into a more strategic role, empowering your team to take on greater responsibilities while you focus on vision, leadership, and innovation. It enables you to create a business that works for you, rather than one that constantly demands your involvement in day-to-day operations. With a solid scaling strategy in place, you can achieve greater work-life balance, financial independence, and the fulfillment that comes from seeing your business grow and thrive.

In summary, scaling is not just about growing bigger – it's about growing smarter. By investing in the right systems, processes, and strategies, you can build a business that is resilient, profitable, and positioned for long-term success. The next sections will provide you with the practical steps and strategies to achieve scalable growth.

## From Operator to CEO: Transitioning to Leadership

For many entrepreneurs, the journey from being deeply involved in the day-to-day operations to becoming a true CEO is both challenging and transformative. In the early stages of a business, it's natural for the founder to be hands-on, managing everything from sales to customer service. However, as the business grows, this operational focus can become a limitation. Achieving successful scaling requires entrepreneurs to undergo a transformative journey, shedding the role of a hands-on operator and embracing the mantle of a visionary CEO. This transition involves a deliberate shift in focus toward crafting a compelling vision, developing robust strategies, and charting a course for sustained, long-term growth.

### *1. Letting Go of Operational Tasks*

The first step in this transition is recognizing that your value as a CEO lies not in managing day-to-day tasks but in leading the company toward its long-term goals. This requires letting go of certain responsibilities and trusting your team to handle them. It can be difficult to relinquish control, especially when you've been involved in every aspect of the business. However, by delegating operational tasks, you free up your time and energy to focus on high-level decision-making and strategic planning.

### *2. Embracing a Leadership Mindset*

Becoming a CEO requires a shift in mindset. Rather than adopting a reactive stance, constantly putting out fires and grappling with daily obstacles, you must cultivate a proactive mindset. This involves diligently anticipating potential challenges, identifying emerging opportunities, and formulating strategic plans to navigate the future landscape of your business. This involves thinking about the big picture, setting the direction for the company, and ensuring that all aspects of the business are aligned with this vision.

### 3. Developing Leadership Skills

As a CEO, your role is not just to manage but to lead. This means developing the skills needed to inspire and motivate your team, make difficult decisions, and navigate the complexities of business growth. Leadership training, mentorship, and continuous learning are essential as you grow into this role.

### 4. Building a Leadership Team

As you transition into the CEO role, it becomes imperative to assemble a robust leadership team to support your vision. This may involve recruiting a skilled Chief Operating Officer (COO) to oversee day-to-day operations, allowing you to focus on strategic initiatives and long-term growth. These are the individuals who will take on the operational responsibilities you once handled, allowing you to focus on leading the company. Hiring and developing a leadership team that shares your vision and values is crucial to scaling your business successfully.

## Strategic Planning: Creating Long-Term Plans Aligned with Vision and Goals.

As a CEO, one of your primary responsibilities is strategic planning. This involves setting long-term goals for the company and developing a plan to achieve them. Strategic planning is about more than just setting targets; it's about aligning every aspect of the business with your vision and ensuring that everyone in the organization is working toward the same objectives.

### 1. Defining Your Vision

The foundation of any strategic plan is a clear and compelling vision for the future of the business. This vision should reflect your long-term aspirations and provide a roadmap for where you want the company to go. It should be ambitious yet achievable, inspiring your team to strive for excellence.

## 2. Setting Strategic Goals

With a clear vision in place, the subsequent step involves establishing strategic objectives designed to propel your organization forward, bringing you closer to realizing your envisioned future. These goals should be specific, measurable, achievable, relevant, and time-bound (SMART). They should cover all areas of the business, from revenue growth and market expansion to product development and customer satisfaction.

## 3. Developing Action Plans

For each strategic goal, develop an action plan that outlines the steps needed to achieve it. This plan should include timelines, resource allocation, and key performance indicators (KPIs) to track progress. It's important to break down long-term goals into smaller, manageable tasks that can be executed by your team.

## 4. Communicating the Plan

The true effectiveness of a strategic plan hinges upon the collective understanding and unwavering commitment of every member of your organization. It is your responsibility as the CEO to ensure that the plan is clearly communicated and that each individual recognizes their role in contributing to its successful execution. As CEO, it's your job to communicate the plan clearly to your team, ensuring that each department and individual knows their role in achieving the company's goals. Regular updates and open communication are essential to keep everyone aligned and motivated.

## 5. Reviewing and Adjusting

Strategic planning is not a one-time activity; it's an ongoing process. Regularly review your progress toward your goals and be prepared to adjust your plan as circumstances change. Whether it's responding to market shifts, seizing new opportunities, or addressing internal challenges, your strategic plan should be flexible enough to adapt to new realities while staying true to your long-term vision.

# Growth Metrics: Tracking Key Metrics to Drive Business Expansion

To scale successfully, it's essential to track the right metrics. Growth metrics provide insight into how well your business is performing and where there are opportunities for improvement. They help you measure progress toward your strategic goals and make data-driven decisions that drive expansion.

### *1. Revenue and Profitability Metrics*

While revenue growth serves as a key indicator of business success, it is essential to recognize that it is not the sole determinant of a thriving enterprise. As you scale, it's important to track both top-line revenue and profitability. This includes metrics like gross profit margin, net profit margin, and customer acquisition cost (CAC). Monitoring these metrics helps you understand how efficiently your business is generating revenue and whether you're on track to achieve your financial goals.

### *2. Customer Metrics*

Customer satisfaction and retention are critical to long-term growth. Key customer metrics include customer lifetime value (CLTV), customer satisfaction score (CSAT), and net promoter score (NPS). These metrics provide insight into how well you're meeting customer needs and how likely customers are to stay with your business and refer others.

### *3. Operational Metrics*

As you scale, operational efficiency becomes increasingly important. Metrics like inventory turnover, order fulfillment time, and employee productivity help you assess how well your operations are running. Identifying areas where efficiency can be improved is key to maintaining profitability as your business grows.

### *4. Market Metrics*

Understanding your position in the market is essential for making strategic decisions. Track market share, competitive analysis, and brand awareness to gauge how well you're performing relative to your competitors. Market metrics can also help you identify new opportunities for expansion or areas where you need to improve.

### *5. Innovation Metrics*

To stay competitive, businesses must continually innovate. Track metrics related to product development, such as the number of new products launched, time to market, and R&D investment. Innovation metrics help ensure that your business is staying ahead of the curve and meeting the evolving needs of your customers.

### *6. Employee Metrics*

Your team is one of your most valuable assets, especially as you scale. Monitor employee satisfaction, retention rates, and training effectiveness to ensure that you're building a strong, motivated workforce. Studies consistently show that high employee engagement is a key driver of productivity and overall business success. Here are some statistics and research findings that highlight the impact of employee engagement:

### *1. Increased Productivity*

According to a Gallup report, highly engaged teams show a 21 percent increase in productivity compared to disengaged teams. Engaged employees are more motivated, take ownership of their work, and are more willing to go above and beyond in their roles, directly impacting business performance.

### *2. Higher Profitability*

Gallup also found that businesses with high employee engagement have 23 percent higher profitability than those with low engagement levels. Engaged employees are more focused and produce higher-quality work, which drives profitability through improved efficiency, innovation, and customer satisfaction.

### *3. Lower Absenteeism and Turnover*

The same Gallup study shows that highly engaged teams experience 41 percent lower absenteeism and a 59 percent lower turnover rate in high-turnover industries. Reduced absenteeism and turnover mean less time and money spent on recruiting, training, and covering for absent employees, which contributes to overall business stability and growth.

### *4. Improved Customer Satisfaction*

A report from Temkin Group found that companies with engaged employees outperform their competitors in customer satisfaction, with customer ratings that are 10 percent higher. Engaged employees tend to provide better customer service, fostering stronger customer loyalty and repeat business.

### *5. Enhanced Innovation*

A study by the University of Warwick found that happy, engaged employees are 12 percent more productive and show greater creativity. This leads to higher levels of innovation, as engaged employees are more likely to bring fresh ideas and problem-solving approaches to the table.

These statistics emphasize that high employee engagement goes beyond individual performance – it contributes to a stronger, more resilient organization with higher productivity, profitability, and customer satisfaction, all of which drive sustainable business success.

### *6. Financial Health Metrics*

Finally, it's important to monitor the overall financial

health of your business. Metrics like cash flow, debt-to-equity ratio, and working capital give you a clear picture of your business's financial stability. These metrics are crucial for making informed decisions about investments, expansion, and risk management.

By tracking these key metrics, you can gain a comprehensive understanding of your business's performance and make strategic decisions that drive growth. Metrics provide the data you need to identify strengths, address weaknesses, and capitalize on opportunities, ensuring that your business is on the path to long-term success.

This chapter guides entrepreneurs through the process of scaling their business by transitioning from operator to CEO, creating strategic plans that align with their vision, and tracking the key metrics that drive growth. By focusing on leadership, strategic planning, and data-driven decision-making, entrepreneurs can position their businesses for sustainable success and continued expansion. Here are some case studies of both success and failure in scaling, highlighting the differences in approaches and outcomes.

## Case Study 1: Amazon – A Blueprint for Successful Scaling.

Background: Amazon started as an online bookstore in 1994, founded by Jeff Bezos in his garage. From its humble beginnings, Amazon has grown into one of the most valuable companies in the world, with diverse business segments ranging from e-commerce and cloud computing to entertainment and logistics.

### *Success Factors*

Visionary Leadership: Jeff Bezos transitioned from being an operator to a CEO with a clear vision for the future. He saw Amazon not just as a bookstore but as "the everything store" that could cater to a global market. Bezos's long-term vision included scaling the business beyond books to encompass a wide range of products and services, which he pursued relentlessly.

Strategic Planning: Amazon's strategic planning involved diversifying its revenue streams, investing in technology (such as the creation of Amazon Web Services), and expanding globally. Bezos focused on growth, even at the expense of short-term profitability, understanding that scale would bring long-term success.

Data-Driven Decision Making: Amazon has always been data-driven, using metrics to track customer behavior, optimize operations, and inform strategic decisions. This approach has allowed Amazon to continually refine its business model, improve efficiency, and stay ahead of competitors.

Outcome: Amazon's success in scaling is evident in its evolution into a global giant with a market capitalization of over a trillion dollars. The company's ability to scale successfully across multiple industries is a testament to the power of visionary leadership, strategic planning, and a relentless focus on data-driven decision-making.

## Case Study 2: Uber – Scaling Rapidly, Facing Growing Pains

Background: Uber, the ride-hailing company, was founded in 2009 and quickly became a global phenomenon. Uber's rapid growth was fueled by its innovative business model, which connected drivers with passengers through a smartphone app.

### Success Factors and Challenges

Aggressive Expansion: Uber's leadership, under co-founder Travis Kalanick, prioritized rapid expansion into new markets. This strategy allowed Uber to quickly dominate the ride-hailing industry and become a household name. However, the company's aggressive approach also led to significant operational challenges.

Scaling Challenges: While Uber scaled quickly, it struggled with maintaining consistent service quality across markets, managing regulatory hurdles, and addressing cultural issues within the company. The company's rapid growth also exposed weaknesses in its leadership and organizational structure.

Leadership Transition: Uber's scaling challenges were compounded by leadership issues. Kalanick's aggressive style led to numerous controversies and legal battles, eventually resulting in his resignation as CEO. The leadership transition was necessary to stabilize the company, but it also highlighted the risks of scaling too quickly without a strong organizational foundation.

Outcome: While Uber successfully scaled to become a global player in the ride-hailing industry, its growth came with significant growing pains. The company has since taken steps to address these challenges under new leadership, focusing on improving its culture, regulatory compliance, and profitability. Uber's story serves as a cautionary tale about the risks of scaling too rapidly without adequate leadership and planning.

## Case Study 3: WeWork – The Dangers of Unsustainable Scaling

Background: WeWork, founded in 2010, was a co-working space company that experienced meteoric growth. Under the leadership of co-founder Adam Neumann, WeWork expanded rapidly, raising billions of dollars in funding and becoming one of the most valuable startups in the world.

### *Failure Factors*

- Lack of Sustainable Business Model: WeWork's aggressive scaling strategy was not matched by a sustainable business model. The company focused on rapid expansion, leasing large amounts of office space and opening new locations at a breakneck pace. However, the underlying economics of the business were flawed, with high operating costs and unproven profitability.

- Leadership and Governance Issues: Adam Neumann's leadership style contributed to WeWork's downfall. His focus on growth at all costs led to reckless decision-making, financial mismanagement, and a lack of oversight. Neumann's extravagant spending and controversial behavior raised concerns among investors and stakeholders.
- Failure to Transition to Sustainable Growth: Despite its initial success, WeWork failed to transition from a high-growth startup to a sustainable business. The company's IPO plans in 2019 unraveled as its financial losses and governance issues came to light. WeWork was forced to scale back its operations, and Neumann stepped down as CEO.

Outcome: WeWork's inability to implement a sustainable scaling strategy precipitated a staggering erosion of its valuation and brought the company to the brink of collapse, underscoring the critical importance of a well-planned and executed approach to growth. While WeWork continues to operate under new leadership, its story serves as a stark reminder of the importance of sustainable growth, sound leadership, and the need for a viable business model when scaling.

## Case Study 4: Netflix – Scaling with Strategic Vision

Background: Netflix started as a DVD rental-by-mail service in 1997, founded by Reed Hastings and Marc Randolph. Over the years, Netflix has transformed into a global streaming service and a major player in content production.

### *Success Factors*

Strategic Vision: Reed Hastings recognized early on that the future of media consumption was online streaming. Netflix's transition from DVD rentals to streaming was a strategic move that positioned the company to scale globally. Hastings' vision extended beyond streaming to include original content production, which has become a cornerstone of Netflix's growth.

Data-Driven Content Decisions: Netflix leverages data analytics to understand viewer preferences and make informed decisions about content production and acquisition. This data-driven approach has allowed Netflix to scale its content library efficiently and cater to diverse audiences across the globe.

International Expansion: Netflix's strategic planning included aggressive international expansion, making its streaming service available in over 190 countries. The company tailored its content offerings to regional preferences, further driving its global growth.

Outcome: Netflix's ability to scale successfully has made it a dominant force in the entertainment industry. The company's focus on strategic vision, data-driven decision-making, and international growth has enabled it to continue expanding while maintaining a strong market position.

## Case Study 5: BlackBerry – Failure to Adapt and Scale

Background: BlackBerry was a leading smartphone brand in the early 2000s, known for its secure email services and physical keyboard. The company's devices were widely used by business professionals and government agencies.

### *Failure Factors*

Inability to Adapt: BlackBerry's leadership failed to recognize the shift in consumer preferences toward touchscreen smartphones, which were popularized by Apple's iPhone. The company clung to its existing product line, believing that its secure email service and physical keyboard would continue to appeal to its core user base.

Lack of Strategic Vision: BlackBerry's strategic planning was shortsighted, focusing on incremental improvements to its existing products rather than innovating and adapting to market changes. The company failed to develop a competitive operating system or app ecosystem, which further hindered its ability to scale.

Operational Inefficiencies: As BlackBerry struggled to compete with iOS and Android devices, it faced operational challenges, including supply chain issues and declining sales. The company's inability to streamline its operations and focus on strategic growth led to a rapid loss of market share.

Outcome: BlackBerry's failure to adapt and scale resulted in a dramatic decline in its market position. The company's once-dominant brand became obsolete as consumers and businesses shifted to more advanced smartphones. BlackBerry's story highlights the dangers of failing to recognize market shifts and the importance of adapting to new technologies when scaling.

## The Lessons of Scaling Success and Failure

These case studies illustrate the critical importance of leadership, strategic planning, and data-driven decision-making in scaling a business. Companies like Amazon and Netflix succeeded in scaling by embracing visionary leadership, setting clear strategic goals, and leveraging data to inform their decisions. On the other hand, companies like WeWork and BlackBerry struggled because they failed to develop sustainable business models, adapt to market changes, and manage their operations effectively.

For entrepreneurs, the key takeaway is that scaling a business requires more than just growth; it requires a thoughtful and strategic approach that aligns with the company's vision and long-term goals. By transitioning from operator to CEO, focusing on strategic growth, and tracking the key metrics that drive success, entrepreneurs can position their businesses for sustainable expansion and long-term success.

Here are reflection questions to help you apply the Scaling and Sustaining Growth lessons to your businesses.

## Readiness for Growth

- Is your business infrastructure ready to support growth? What areas need strengthening?
- How can you build a scalable model that doesn't rely solely on your involvement?

## Team and Resource Management

- Do you have the right team and resources in place to support growth?
- How can you foster a culture of growth and innovation within your team?

## Setting Scalable Goals

- What are the top three goals for scaling your business in the next year?
- How will these goals support your long-term vision for sustainable growth?

# CHAPTER 8:
# FUTURE-PROOFING YOUR BUSINESS

*"To be successful, you have to have your heart in your business, and your business in your heart."*
– Thomas J. Watson

In today's rapidly evolving business landscape, maintaining a keen awareness of potential market shifts is essential for long-term success and sustainability. Being able to identify and respond to early warning signs allows you to make strategic adjustments, adapt quickly, and prevent negative impacts on your business. This section provides key indicators to watch for and actionable steps to prepare for market shifts before they become challenges.

## Key Early Warning Signs to Watch For

### Shifts in Customer Behavior

- Indicator: Decreased engagement, changes in purchasing patterns, or new customer demands.
- Action: Conduct frequent customer surveys and analyze feedback to gain valuable insights into evolving preferences, needs, and pain points, enabling you to stay ahead of the curve and adapt your offerings accordingly.

### Competitor Actions

- Indicator: Competitors adopting new technologies,

expanding services, or launching aggressive marketing campaigns.
- Action: Set up competitor monitoring to track major moves in the industry. Use tools like Google Alerts, social media listening, or competitive analysis reports to stay updated.

## *Technological Advancements*

- Indicator: Emerging technologies disrupting existing processes or customer expectations.
- Action: Stay informed about technological advancements by actively participating in industry conferences, subscribing to curated tech newsletters, and engaging with thought leaders and innovators on professional networking platforms like LinkedIn.

## *Regulatory Changes*

- Indicator: Announcements of new laws, standards, or regulations that may affect your industry.
- Action: Stay informed by subscribing to industry news and government updates. Engage with trade associations or legal advisors to understand and prepare for potential regulatory shifts.

## *Economic Trends*

- Indicator: Market downturns, interest rate fluctuations, or changes in consumer spending power.
- Action: Monitor economic indicators relevant to your industry, such as consumer confidence indexes, employment rates, and inflation. By gaining a comprehensive understanding of the broader economic landscape, you can make informed decisions about resource allocation, investments, and strategic planning, enabling you to anticipate potential risks and implement effective mitigation strategies

proactively.

***Supplier or Partner Instability***

- Indicator: Disruptions in your supply chain, rising costs from vendors, or unreliable partnerships.
- Action: Diversify suppliers, seek backup partnerships, and maintain open communication with current vendors. Cultivating a more agile and diversified supply chain not only mitigates the risk of over-reliance on a single supplier but also enhances your business's resilience in the face of unforeseen disruptions, ensuring continuity and adaptability.

## Specific Action Items for Future-Proofing Your Business

Future-proofing your business requires a proactive approach that focuses on cultivating resilience, embracing adaptability, and developing strategic foresight to navigate the complexities of an ever-changing market. Here are targeted action items to ensure your business remains robust and agile, regardless of market fluctuations.

### *1. Invest in Continuous Learning and Development*

- Action: Encourage your team to upskill by offering training programs and access to online courses. Stay informed about industry trends, emerging technologies, and new business practices to keep your company competitive.
- Outcome: An informed and skilled team that adapts quickly to changes and brings fresh ideas to the table.

### *2. Diversify Revenue Streams*

- Action: Explore additional products, services, or markets that complement your core business. For instance, consider offering digital services, launching a subscription model, or expanding into

adjacent markets.
- Outcome: Reduced dependency on a single revenue source, protecting your business from sector-specific downturns.

### *3. Develop Scenario Planning Exercises*

- Action: Use scenario planning to envision potential future events and devise response strategies. Create best-case, worst-case, and moderate scenarios to understand how each would impact your business.
- Outcome: A proactive mindset and an adaptable plan, allowing your team to act quickly in any situation.

### *4. Build a Cash Reserve*

- Action: Set aside a percentage of profits each month to build a financial cushion. Aim for a reserve that can cover three to six months of operating expenses.
- Outcome: Financial flexibility to weather unexpected expenses or revenue fluctuations without resorting to layoffs or cost-cutting measures that may weaken the business.

### *5. Strengthen Digital and Online Presence*

- Action: Invest in a robust digital marketing strategy, improve your website's functionality, and build active social media profiles. Expand your online customer support to meet the demands of a digital-first consumer base.
- Outcome: A strong digital footprint that broadens reach and builds brand loyalty, ensuring business visibility even as customer behavior shifts online.

### *6. Build a Flexible Workforce Model*

- Action: Consider a mix of full-time employees,

freelancers, and consultants to adjust staffing levels according to demand. Encourage remote work options and flexible hours to attract a broader talent pool.
- Outcome: An adaptable workforce that can scale up or down quickly, giving you the ability to respond to changes in demand without major disruptions.

## *7. Embrace Data-Driven Decision-Making*

- Action: Invest in analytics tools that provide real-time data on key metrics (e.g., sales, customer engagement, or supply chain performance). Encourage team members to use data for decision-making and problem-solving.
- Outcome: Greater accuracy and responsiveness, as data insights help you make informed decisions that align with both current and future business goals.

## *8. Foster a Culture of Innovation*

- Action: Encourage employees to share ideas for improvement and innovation. Implement a feedback system and reward creative problem-solving that aligns with business objectives.
- Outcome: A culture that supports forward-thinking and experimentation, helping the business stay ahead of the curve.

## Building a Future-Ready Business

By proactively identifying early warning signs and implementing future-proofing strategies, you can build a resilient business that not only survives but thrives amidst market changes. Being prepared means equipping yourself and your team with the tools, flexibility, and foresight needed to tackle challenges head-on. With these action items in place, your business will be positioned to capitalize on opportunities, mitigate risks, and maintain its course, no matter the market shifts that come your way. The above action steps provide you with a practical guide to early warning signs and actionable steps to protect your business in the long term.

This chapter encourages entrepreneurs to future-proof their businesses by staying ahead of market trends, committing to lifelong learning, and building a legacy that transcends immediate profits. By focusing on sustainability, social responsibility, and long-term vision, entrepreneurs can create businesses that not only succeed in the present but also leave a lasting impact for future generations.

## Staying Ahead of the Curve: Assessing and Adapting to New Technologies and Market Trends

In an era marked by unprecedented change and disruption, staying ahead of the curve has transitioned from being a mere competitive advantage to becoming an absolute imperative for business survival and long-term success. The relentless pace of technological advancement and the incessant fluctuations in market dynamics demand that businesses embrace agility and adopt a forward-thinking mindset to maintain their competitive edge and thrive in an increasingly complex and unpredictable business environment. Future-proofing your business involves continuously assessing emerging technologies and market trends and adapting your strategies accordingly.

Regular Market Analysis: To stay ahead, it's essential to regularly analyze market trends and shifts in consumer behavior. This involves keeping an eye on your industry, understanding the macroeconomic factors that could impact your business, and identifying potential disruptors. Market analysis should be an ongoing process integrated into your strategic planning to ensure that your business is always ready to pivot when necessary.

Embracing New Technologies: Technological advancements can provide businesses with new tools to enhance efficiency, improve customer experience, and open new revenue streams. Whether it's artificial intelligence, blockchain, or the latest in automation, being open to adopting new technologies can give your business a competitive edge. However, it's important to carefully assess the ROI of new technologies and ensure they align with your business goals before implementing them. Here's a specific example of how technological advancements can transform a business:

PureBlend, a small chain of smoothie and juice bars, initially operated with a simple cash register system, paper-based inventory tracking, and in-person-only ordering. As the business grew, the owner recognized the limitations of these outdated processes in meeting customer demands efficiently. To improve operations, customer experience, and revenue, PureBlend decided to invest in technology-driven solutions:

1. Efficiency through POS and Inventory Management: PureBlend implemented a cloud-based POS (Point of Sale) system that integrated inventory management. This allowed the team to track ingredient levels in real-time, reducing the risk of running out of key ingredients during peak hours. The system also automated ordering when stocks were low, ensuring the team could maintain consistent service. This reduced inventory costs by 15 percent and minimized waste from over-ordering.
2. Enhanced Customer Experience with a Mobile App: PureBlend launched a branded mobile app where customers could place orders for pick-up, customize their smoothies, and save favorite orders. The app offered a seamless experience that allowed busy customers to skip lines, while the in-app loyalty program rewarded repeat customers with discounts and exclusive offers. As a result, customer satisfaction scores increased by 20 percent, and in-app orders accounted for 30 percent of total sales within six months.
3. New Revenue Stream with Delivery and Subscription Services: The app allowed PureBlend to

introduce delivery services, reaching customers beyond their physical store locations. Additionally, they launched a subscription model for their most popular smoothies, allowing customers to sign up for weekly deliveries. This new revenue stream brought in an additional 10 percent increase in monthly sales, appealing to health-conscious customers who appreciated the convenience.

Results: By embracing technology, PureBlend was able to streamline operations, improve customer satisfaction, and diversify its revenue sources. The efficiencies gained allowed employees to focus more on customer service, and the new app and delivery services attracted a broader customer base. Within a year, PureBlend's revenue grew by 25 percent, driven by a combination of improved in-store efficiency, increased customer loyalty, and new delivery and subscription sales.

This example demonstrates how technological advancements can help businesses enhance efficiency, elevate the customer experience, and create new avenues for growth.

Innovation as a Core Value: Making innovation a core value of your business can help ensure that you're always looking for ways to improve and stay ahead. Encourage a culture of creativity and experimentation within your team, where new ideas are welcomed and tested. This proactive approach to innovation can help you identify new opportunities and stay relevant in a constantly changing market.

Strategic Flexibility: One of the keys to staying ahead of the curve is maintaining strategic flexibility. This means being willing to change course when necessary and not getting too attached to existing products, services, or business models. The most successful businesses are those that can quickly adapt to new realities, whether that means pivoting to a new market, adopting new technology, or rethinking their value proposition.

## Continuous Learning: Lifelong Learning and Staying Informed

In an age of rapid change, continuous learning is crucial for both personal and business success. The world is evolving at an unprecedented pace, and what worked yesterday may not be effective tomorrow. Entrepreneurs who commit to lifelong learning are better equipped to navigate these changes, seize new opportunities, and lead their businesses to success.

Staying Informed: To stay ahead, you must stay informed. This means regularly reading industry publications, attending conferences, participating in webinars, and engaging with thought leaders in your field. By keeping up with the latest developments in your industry, you can anticipate changes and position your business to take advantage of them.

Professional Development: Continuous learning isn't just about staying informed; it's also about developing new skills. Whether it's learning about new technologies, improving your leadership abilities, or gaining a deeper understanding of market dynamics, investing in your professional development is essential. Consider enrolling in courses, seeking out mentorship, or joining industry groups to expand your knowledge and skill set.

Encouraging Learning Within Your Team: As a leader, it's important to foster a culture of continuous learning within your organization. Encourage your team to pursue professional development opportunities and provide them with the resources they need to do so. A well-educated and skilled team is a major asset in adapting to change and driving innovation.

Embracing a Growth Mindset: Adopting a growth mindset – believing that abilities and intelligence can be developed through dedication and hard work – is essential for continuous learning. Entrepreneurs with a growth mindset are more likely to embrace challenges, persist in the face of setbacks, and see effort as the path to mastery. This mindset not only benefits you personally but also sets a positive example for your team.

## Building a Legacy: Thinking Beyond Immediate Profits

As an entrepreneur, it's easy to get caught up in the day-to-day demands of running a business and the pursuit of immediate profits. However, truly successful entrepreneurs think beyond the short term and consider the long-term impact of their decisions. Building a legacy involves creating a business that not only generates profit but also makes a positive impact on the world and endures for generations.

1. Defining Your Legacy: Building a legacy starts with defining what you want your business to stand for. This goes beyond financial success to include the values, principles, and mission that guide your company. Ask yourself: What do you want your business to be known for? How do you want to be remembered as a leader? These questions can help you define the legacy you want to create.
2. Sustainable Growth: Sustainable growth is key to building a lasting legacy. This means making decisions that prioritize long-term success over short-term gains. It involves investing in the health and well-being of your employees, building strong relationships with customers and partners, and contributing positively to your community and the environment. A focus on sustainability ensures that your business will continue to thrive for years to come.
3. Social Responsibility: Entrepreneurs who leave an indelible mark on their industries and society often achieve this by weaving social responsibility into the very fabric of their business models, ensuring that their organizations generate not only financial returns but also meaningful, positive impact on the

communities they serve and the world at large. This could involve adopting environmentally friendly practices, supporting charitable causes, or creating products and services that improve people's lives. By contributing to the greater good, you create a legacy that goes beyond profit and has a lasting impact on society.
4. Succession Planning: A crucial aspect of crafting an enduring legacy is putting in place the necessary structures, processes, and talent development initiatives to ensure that your business can maintain its trajectory of success and continue to embody your vision and values long after you have passed the torch to the next generation of leaders. Succession planning involves identifying and developing future leaders within your organization who can carry on your vision and values. A well-thought-out succession plan ensures that your business remains strong and stable, even as leadership transitions over time.
5. Long-Term Vision: Ultimately, building a legacy requires a long-term vision. This means thinking about where you want your business to be in ten, twenty, or even fifty years. It's about setting goals that extend beyond your tenure and laying the groundwork for future generations to build upon. By keeping your eye on the long term, you can make decisions today that will benefit your business and the world for years to come.

This chapter encourages entrepreneurs to future-proof their businesses by staying ahead of market trends, committing to lifelong learning, and building a legacy that transcends immediate profits. By focusing on sustainability, social responsibility, and long-term vision, entrepreneurs can create businesses that not only succeed in the present but also leave a lasting impact for future generations. Here are some relevant case studies that illustrate these principles in action.

## Case Study 1: Patagonia – Building a Legacy Through Sustainability

Background: Patagonia, founded by Yvon Chouinard in 1973, is an outdoor apparel company that has built its brand around environmental sustainability and social responsibility. From the beginning, Patagonia has been committed to reducing its environmental footprint and advocating for the preservation of natural resources.

### *Future-Proofing Strategies*

1. Sustainability and Environmental Activism: Patagonia has made sustainability a core part of its business model. The company uses recycled materials in its products, advocates for environmental causes, and donates a percentage of its profits to environmental organizations. Patagonia's "Worn Wear" program encourages customers to repair and recycle their clothing, reducing waste and promoting sustainable consumption.
2. Social Responsibility: Patagonia has been vocal about social and environmental issues, taking bold stances on climate change, public lands protection, and fair labor practices. The company's commitment to social responsibility has resonated with consumers, building strong brand loyalty and trust.
3. Long-Term Vision: Patagonia's long-term vision is to be in business for the planet. The company's mission statement, "We're in business to save our home planet," reflects its dedication to environmental stewardship and its desire to leave a positive legacy for future generations.

Impact: Patagonia's focus on sustainability, social responsibility, and long-term vision has not only driven its success but has also set a standard for other businesses to follow. The company has built a loyal customer base that values its ethical practices, and its brand is synonymous with environmental activism. Patagonia's legacy as a leader in sustainability continues to grow, influencing industries far beyond outdoor apparel.

## Case Study 2: Unilever – Sustainable Growth and Social Impact

Background: Unilever, a global consumer goods company, has embraced sustainability and social responsibility as central pillars of its business strategy. With a portfolio of brands that includes Dove, Ben & Jerry's, and Hellmann's, Unilever has made a significant impact on the global market by integrating sustainability into its core operations.

### *Future-Proofing Strategies*

1. Sustainable Living Plan: Unilever's Sustainable Living Plan, launched in 2010, set ambitious goals to reduce the company's environmental footprint, improve health and well-being, and enhance livelihoods. The plan focuses on areas such as reducing greenhouse gas emissions, improving water and waste management, and sourcing 100 percent of its agricultural raw materials sustainably.

2. Social Responsibility and Brand Purpose: Unilever has focused on building brands with purpose, aligning each brand with social or environmental causes. For example, Dove's "Real Beauty" campaign promotes body positivity, while Ben & Jerry's advocates for climate justice and social equity. This approach has helped Unilever connect with consumers on a deeper level, driving brand loyalty and differentiation.

3. Long-Term Vision: Unilever's long-term vision is to grow its business while decoupling its environmental impact from its growth. The company has committed to reducing its environmental footprint by half while continuing to expand its global operations. Unilever's leadership believes that

sustainable business practices are essential for long-term success and that businesses have a responsibility to contribute positively to society.

Impact: Unilever's commitment to sustainability and social responsibility has positioned the company as a leader in the consumer goods industry. The Sustainable Living Plan has delivered significant environmental and social benefits while also driving business growth. Unilever's focus on building brands with purpose has resonated with consumers, helping the company achieve sustainable success and create a legacy.

## Case Study 3: Tesla – Driving Innovation and Sustainability in the Automotive Industry

Background: Tesla, founded by Elon Musk in 2003, has revolutionized the automotive industry with its electric vehicles (EVs) and commitment to sustainable energy. Tesla's mission is to accelerate the world's transition to sustainable energy, and the company has consistently pushed the boundaries of innovation to achieve this goal.

### *Future-Proofing Strategies*

Sustainability and Renewable Energy: Tesla's core business is built around sustainability, with a focus on electric vehicles, solar energy, and energy storage solutions. The company's EVs have helped reduce carbon emissions and promote the adoption of renewable energy. Tesla's solar products, including solar panels and Solar Roof, further support the company's mission to promote sustainable energy solutions.

Innovation and Technological Leadership: Tesla has consistently led the industry in innovation, from the development of cutting-edge battery technology to the creation of autonomous driving systems. The company's focus on continuous improvement and technological advancement has kept it ahead of competitors and allowed it to scale rapidly.

Long-Term Vision: Tesla's long-term vision extends beyond cars to creating a sustainable energy ecosystem. The company's focus on integrating EVs, solar energy, and energy storage solutions positions it to lead the transition to a more sustainable future. Tesla's Gigafactories, which produce batteries at scale, are a key component of this vision, driving down costs and increasing accessibility to sustainable energy.

Impact: Tesla's relentless pursuit of sustainability and groundbreaking innovation has propelled it to the forefront of the automotive and energy sectors, revolutionizing the way we think about transportation and clean energy, and catalyzing a global shift towards a more sustainable future. The company's products have transformed how consumers think about transportation and energy, setting a new standard for environmental responsibility. Tesla's long-term vision for a sustainable future continues to drive its growth and influence, ensuring its legacy as a pioneer in sustainable technology.

## Case Study 4: IKEA – Sustainability and Affordable Living

Background: IKEA, the Swedish furniture and home goods retailer, is known for its affordable, flat-pack furniture and its commitment to sustainability. Founded in 1943, IKEA has grown into a global brand with a strong focus on reducing its environmental impact and promoting sustainable living.

### *Future-Proofing Strategies*

1. Sustainable Sourcing and Circular Economy: IKEA has committed to sourcing 100 percent of its wood, cotton, and other materials from sustainable sources. The company is also focused on creating a circular economy, where products are designed for reuse, refurbishment, and recycling. IKEA's "Buy Back" program allows customers to return used

furniture, which is then resold or recycled, reducing waste.
2. Energy Efficiency and Renewable Energy: IKEA has invested heavily in renewable energy, with the goal of becoming energy independent. The company operates wind farms and solar installations, and it offers energy-efficient products such as LED lighting. IKEA's stores are designed to minimize energy use, and the company has committed to reducing its carbon footprint across its supply chain.
3. Long-Term Vision: IKEA's long-term vision is to create a better everyday life for people while minimizing its impact on the planet. The company's focus on sustainability, affordability, and innovation aligns with its vision of making sustainable living accessible to everyone.

Impact: IKEA's commitment to sustainability and affordable living has made it a leader in the retail industry. The company's efforts to promote a circular economy and reduce its environmental impact have resonated with consumers, driving brand loyalty and growth. IKEA's long-term vision ensures that it will continue to be a force for positive change in the world, creating a legacy for future generations.

## Case Study 5: Danone – Integrating Social Responsibility into Business Growth

Background: Danone, a multinational food-products corporation, has made sustainability and social responsibility central to its business strategy. The company's mission is to bring health through food to as many people as possible while also contributing to environmental sustainability and social progress.

### *Future-Proofing Strategies*

1. One Planet. One Health Initiative: Danone's "One Planet. One Health" initiative emphasizes the

interconnectedness of human health and the health of the planet. The company focuses on sustainable sourcing, reducing greenhouse gas emissions, and promoting biodiversity. Danone also supports regenerative agriculture practices to improve soil health and protect ecosystems.

2. B Corp Certification: Danone has committed to becoming a certified B Corporation, which means it meets rigorous standards of social and environmental performance, accountability, and transparency. This certification aligns with Danone's commitment to social responsibility and its long-term vision of creating a positive impact on society.
3. Inclusive Growth: Danone is dedicated to promoting inclusive growth by supporting local communities, improving access to nutrition, and fostering diversity and inclusion within its workforce. The company works closely with smallholder farmers and local suppliers to create sustainable supply chains and support economic development.

Impact: Danone's integration of sustainability and social responsibility into its business strategy has strengthened its brand and contributed to its global success. The company's commitment to building a healthier world through sustainable practices and social impact has positioned it as a leader in the food industry. Danone's long-term vision ensures that it will continue to drive positive change and create a lasting legacy for future generations.

## The Power of Futureproofing Through Vision, Sustainability, and Social Responsibility

These case studies highlight the importance of futureproofing a business by staying ahead of market trends, committing to lifelong learning, and building a legacy that transcends immediate profits. Companies like Patagonia, Unilever, Tesla, IKEA, and Danone have successfully integrated sustainability, social responsibility, and long-term vision into their business strategies. By doing so, they have not only achieved success in the present but have also positioned themselves to leave a lasting impact on the world.

Here are reflection questions to help readers apply the lessons from Building a Resilient Business to your businesses.

## Reflection Questions

### *Identifying Risks and Vulnerabilities*

- What are the biggest risks your business faces? Are these primarily internal or external?
- How have you prepared for potential disruptions (e.g., market changes, economic downturns)?

### *Resilience Planning*

- What measures can you implement to strengthen your business's resilience?
- Are there areas where you can diversify or improve flexibility to reduce reliance on a single revenue stream?

### *Assessing Adaptability*

- How well does your team respond to change?
- How can you cultivate a culture of adaptability and resilience among your employees?

# CHAPTER 9:
# THE ENTREPRENEUR'S JOURNEY

*"If your actions inspire others to dream more,
learn more, do more, and become more, you are a leader."*

– John Quincy Adams

## Reflecting on the Transformation: From Operator to True Entrepreneur

As we conclude this journey through the essentials of entrepreneurial success, it's important to reflect on the transformation you've undergone – from being an operator immersed in the daily grind to becoming a true entrepreneur and visionary leader. Transitioning from the management of daily tasks to a focus on long-term growth is a challenging yet essential step in scaling your business and unlocking its true potential.

In the beginning, like many entrepreneurs, you may have found yourself wearing multiple hats, involved in every aspect of your business. This hands-on approach, while necessary in the early stages, can quickly become a hindrance as your business grows. Embracing the role of CEO – a position that demands leadership, strategic thinking, and innovation – necessitates a profound shift in both mindset and behavior. It involves letting go of operational tasks, delegating responsibilities, and trusting your team to manage the day-to-day operations.

This journey from operator to entrepreneur is marked

by a shift in focus: from the immediate to the strategic. To maintain a competitive edge, it is imperative that you cultivate a mindset of agility and openness to change, allowing you to adapt swiftly to new circumstances and capitalize on emerging opportunities. It's about moving beyond the details and seeing the bigger picture, understanding where your business is headed, and steering it in the right direction. This transformation allows you to create a sustainable business that can adapt, grow, and thrive in an ever-changing market.

## The Ongoing Journey: Embracing Continuous Evolution

While this book has guided you through key steps in your entrepreneurial journey, it's important to remember that the journey doesn't end here. Entrepreneurship is an ongoing process of learning, adapting, and evolving. As your business grows, so must your skills, strategies, and vision.

The business landscape is dynamic, with new challenges and opportunities emerging all the time. To stay ahead, you must remain agile and open to change. This means continually assessing your business, embracing new technologies, and refining your strategies. It also means being willing to pivot when necessary, to explore new markets, and to innovate in ways that keep your business relevant and competitive.

Your role as an entrepreneur will also continue to evolve. As your business scales, you may find yourself stepping into new roles – whether that's expanding your leadership team, entering new markets, or even mentoring the next generation of entrepreneurs. Embrace this evolution as a natural part of your journey and stay committed to your growth as a leader.

Remember, the most successful entrepreneurs are those who view their journey as a marathon, not a sprint. They understand that continuous improvement, learning, and adaptation are key to long-term success. By staying curious, open-minded, and forward-thinking, you can navigate the challenges that come your way and lead your business to new heights.

## Final Thoughts: The Importance of Vision, Innovation, and Leadership

As we close this book, I want to leave you with three key principles that are essential for achieving long-term success as an entrepreneur: vision, innovation, and leadership.

Vision: Your vision serves as the bedrock upon which your business is built, providing a guiding light for your decisions, igniting the passion of your team, and establishing the essence of your brand. A clear and compelling vision provides direction and purpose, helping you stay focused on your long-term goals even in the face of challenges. Never lose sight of your vision, and always strive to align your actions with it.

Innovation: In today's fast-paced world, innovation is not just a competitive advantage – it's a necessity. To stay relevant and ahead of the curve, you must be willing to embrace new ideas, experiment with new technologies, and continuously improve your products, services, and processes. Foster an organizational culture that thrives on innovation, one in which creativity is not only encouraged but celebrated, and calculated risks are embraced as necessary steps on the path to growth.

Leadership: Finally, leadership is the glue that holds everything together. As an entrepreneur, your ability to lead effectively – whether it's inspiring your team, making tough decisions, or navigating through uncertainty – is what will ultimately determine your success. Great leaders are those who lead by example, communicate their vision clearly, and empower their teams to achieve their best. Dedicate time and resources to your own growth as a leader, continuously working to embody the qualities of a leader who inspires, empowers, and elevates those around them to achieve their highest potential.

The journey of an entrepreneur is one of continuous transformation, learning, and growth. By embracing your role as a visionary leader, fostering a culture of innovation, and staying true to your long-term vision, you can build a business that not only succeeds but also makes a lasting impact. The road ahead may be challenging, but it is also filled with opportunities to create, innovate, and lead in ways that shape the future. Embrace this journey with passion and purpose, and the rewards will be beyond measure.

This chapter encapsulates the essence of the entrepreneurial journey, emphasizing the transition from operator to true entrepreneur, the importance of continuous evolution, and the critical roles that vision, innovation, and leadership play in achieving long-term success. It serves as both a conclusion and a motivational call to action, encouraging entrepreneurs to keep pushing forward and striving for excellence in all they do. Below are some business case studies that illustrate these themes and provide valuable lessons for entrepreneurs on their journey.

## Case Study 1: Microsoft – The Power of Vision and Innovation

Background: Microsoft, founded by Bill Gates and Paul Allen in 1975, became a dominant player in the software industry with its Windows operating system and Office suite. However, by the early 2000s, Microsoft was facing significant challenges as it struggled to adapt to the rise of the internet, mobile computing, and cloud technologies.

Entrepreneurial Transition: Under the leadership of Satya Nadella, who became CEO in 2014, Microsoft underwent a significant transformation. Nadella emphasized the importance of innovation, cloud computing, and a renewed focus on customer-centricity. He steered Microsoft away from its legacy focus on Windows and toward new growth areas, such as Azure cloud services, AI, and enterprise solutions.

Vision and Leadership: Nadella's vision for Microsoft was centered on empowering every person and organization on the planet to achieve more. He fostered a culture of continuous learning, collaboration, and inclusivity, encouraging employees to embrace a growth mindset. This shift in leadership and vision revitalized Microsoft, making it one of the most valuable companies in the world.

Outcome: Microsoft's transition under Nadella's leadership demonstrates the power of vision, innovation, and continuous evolution. Microsoft's strategic transition to cloud computing is exemplified by the evolution of its Office suite into Microsoft 365. Traditionally, Office applications like Word, Excel, and PowerPoint were sold as one-time purchases, requiring users to buy new versions for updates. Recognizing the shift towards cloud services, Microsoft introduced Microsoft 365, a subscription-based model offering continuous updates, cloud storage via OneDrive, and collaborative tools like Teams. This transformation not only provided users with up-to-date software but also integrated cloud-based features, enhancing productivity and collaboration. As a result, Microsoft 365 has become a cornerstone of Microsoft's cloud strategy, significantly contributing to the company's growth and aligning with modern computing trends. By embracing change and focusing on long-term growth areas, Microsoft not only regained its competitive edge but also set a new standard for leadership in the tech industry.

## Case Study 2: IBM – Reinventing Through Continuous Evolution

Background: IBM, founded in 1911, has a long history of innovation, from developing the first mainframe computers to pioneering artificial intelligence with its Watson platform. However, like many legacy technology companies, IBM faced challenges as the tech landscape evolved, particularly with the rise of cloud computing and AI.

Entrepreneurial Transition: IBM's leadership recognized

the need to evolve and reinvent the company to stay relevant in a rapidly changing industry. The company shifted its focus from traditional hardware and software to cloud computing, AI, and blockchain technologies. IBM also acquired companies like Red Hat to strengthen its cloud offerings and provide integrated solutions to enterprise clients.

Vision and Leadership: IBM's vision has always been rooted in innovation and the belief that technology can drive progress and improve the world. The company's leadership embraced this vision by focusing on emerging technologies and adapting its business model to meet the needs of modern enterprises. IBM's commitment to research and development has kept it at the forefront of technological innovation.

Outcome: IBM's capacity for continuous evolution and adaptation in the face of shifting market dynamics has been the key to its enduring success, enabling the company to maintain its position as a prominent force in the technology sector for more than a hundred years. The company's focus on innovation and leadership has ensured its long-term success and relevance in a highly competitive landscape.

## Case Study 3: Walt Disney – The Importance of Vision and Leadership

Background: Walt Disney, founded by Walt and Roy Disney in 1923, began as an animation studio and quickly became a household name with the creation of iconic characters like Mickey Mouse. Over the decades, Disney expanded into theme parks, television, and film, becoming a global entertainment powerhouse.

Entrepreneurial Transition: Walt Disney was a visionary leader who constantly pushed the boundaries of what was possible in entertainment. His willingness to take risks and innovate, such as creating the first synchronized sound cartoon and building Disneyland, set the stage for Disney's long-term success. After Walt's death, the company faced challenges, but subsequent leaders like Michael Eisner and

Bob Iger continued to drive Disney's evolution through acquisitions and expansion into new markets.

Vision and Leadership: Walt Disney's vision centered on the creation of a unique space where families could come together to experience the magic of entertainment, regardless of the medium – be it through the wonder of movies, the enchantment of theme parks, or the joy of television. This vision has guided the company's growth and diversification. Under Bob Iger's leadership, Disney acquired Pixar, Marvel, Lucasfilm, and 21st Century Fox, significantly expanding its content portfolio and solidifying its position as a leader in the entertainment industry.

Outcome: Disney's journey from a small animation studio to a global entertainment empire illustrates the importance of vision, innovation, and leadership. The company's ability to evolve and expand into new areas has allowed it to maintain its legacy as a beloved brand while continuing to achieve long-term success.

## Case Study 4: Nike – From Operator to Visionary Brand

Background: Nike, founded by Bill Bowerman and Phil Knight in 1964, started as a distributor of Japanese running shoes. Over time, the company developed its own line of footwear, eventually becoming the world's leading sportswear brand.

Entrepreneurial Transition: Phil Knight's transition from operator to visionary leader was marked by his ability to recognize and capitalize on cultural trends in sports and fitness. Knight focused on building a brand that was not just about selling shoes but about inspiring athletes and promoting an active lifestyle. Nike's iconic "Just Do It" campaign and partnerships with athletes like Michael Jordan transformed the company into a global brand.

Vision and Leadership: Nike's vision has always been to bring inspiration and innovation to every athlete in the world. Knight's leadership emphasized the importance of brand identity, innovation in product design, and strategic marketing. Nike's investments in technology, such as the development of Nike Air and Flyknit, further solidified its reputation as an innovator in sportswear.

Outcome: Nike's evolution from a shoe distributor to a global brand leader demonstrates the power of visionary leadership and strategic growth. The company's focus on innovation, brand identity, and market expansion has driven its long-term success and established Nike as a cultural icon.

## Case Study 5: Kodak – The Consequences of Failing to Evolve

Background: Kodak, once the dominant player in the photography industry, was founded in 1888 by George Eastman. The company revolutionized photography by making it accessible to the public, but it failed to adapt to the digital revolution.

Entrepreneurial Stagnation: Despite inventing the first digital camera in 1975, Kodak's leadership was slow to transition from film to digital photography. The company continued to focus on its traditional film business, underestimating the impact of digital technology on the industry. Kodak's reluctance to innovate and evolve with changing market trends led to a steady decline in its market position.

Lack of Vision and Leadership: Kodak's inability to adapt to the digital revolution stemmed from a myopic leadership approach that placed a higher value on immediate financial gains than on the long-term benefits of embracing technological innovation. The company's inability to envision a future beyond film ultimately led to its downfall. In 2012, Kodak filed for bankruptcy, marking the end of an era for a once-dominant brand.

Outcome: Kodak's story serves as a cautionary tale of what can happen when a company fails to evolve and adapt to new technologies. The lack of visionary leadership and an unwillingness to embrace change led to the demise of a company that had once been an industry leader. The cautionary tale of Kodak serves as a stark reminder of the paramount importance of continuous evolution and a relentless pursuit of innovation in securing a company's long-term success and viability.

Conclusion: These case studies illustrate the critical importance of transitioning from operator to true entrepreneur, embracing continuous evolution, and the roles that vision, innovation, and leadership play in achieving long-term success. Companies like Microsoft, Disney, Nike, and IBM have thrived by evolving their business models, fostering innovation, and maintaining a clear vision for the future. On the other hand, Kodak's failure to adapt highlights the risks of stagnation and the importance of continuous evolution.

As you continue your entrepreneurial journey, these examples serve as a powerful reminder that success requires more than just operational excellence. Lasting success necessitates an unwavering dedication to growth, a readiness to welcome change as an opportunity rather than an obstacle, and the foresight to look past the challenges of the present moment and envision a brighter future. By focusing on these principles, you can build a business that not only succeeds in the present but also leaves a lasting impact for future generations. Keep pushing forward, stay true to your vision, and continue to strive for excellence in all that you do. The journey of entrepreneurship is one of constant learning, adaptation, and growth – and the rewards are well worth the effort.

Here are reflection questions to help you apply the Developing Your Leadership Legacy lessons to your business.

## Vision for Legacy

- What kind of legacy do you want to leave within your business and industry?
- Are there specific values or goals you want to ensure are sustained in the future?

## Leadership Development

- How are you actively investing in and developing future leaders within your company?
- Who on your team could carry forward the values and mission of your business?

## Defining Your Legacy Goals

- What specific achievements or changes would make you feel proud of your leadership legacy?
- How can you start building that legacy today, even in small ways?

# CHAPTER 10:
# A FINAL WISH FOR YOUR ENTREPRENEURIAL JOURNEY

*"The best way to predict the future is to invent it."*
– Alan Kay

Your role as a visionary is the most important aspect of your entrepreneurial journey. It is your vision that sets the direction for your business, inspires your team, and drives the growth that will transform your company from a small startup into a thriving, medium-sized enterprise – and perhaps even into a Fortune 500 company. Your vision serves as a guiding light, keeping you focused on the broader landscape and ensuring that each decision you make is a strategic step toward realizing the long-term objectives you've established for your venture.

This chapter serves as a heartfelt wish for you, the reader, encouraging you to fully embrace your role as a visionary leader, to delegate responsibilities, and to implement the strategies discussed throughout this book. As you continue your entrepreneurial journey, remember that your success is not just about building a profitable business – it's about creating value for all stakeholders and building a legacy that will endure for generations.

To help you on this path, here are some key lessons and principles that successful entrepreneurs abide by, along with examples of how these have played out in real-world scenarios.

## 1. Embrace Visionary Leadership: Steve Jobs and Apple

Lesson: A clear and compelling vision is the cornerstone of successful leadership. It's what inspires your team, guides your decisions, and drives your business forward.

Steve Jobs exemplifies the transformative power of visionary leadership, demonstrating how a clear and compelling vision can revolutionize industries and shape the course of modern business.

Principle: Maintain an unwavering commitment to your long-term vision, allowing it to serve as the compass that guides each decision you make, ensuring that your actions consistently align with your overarching goals. Your vision should inspire your team and give them a sense of purpose beyond the day-to-day tasks.

## 2. Delegate to Elevate: Howard Schultz and Starbucks

Lesson: Delegating responsibilities is crucial to scaling your business. As a leader, you must focus on strategic growth and let your team handle the operations.

Example: Howard Schultz, the former CEO of Starbucks, understood the importance of delegating operational tasks to focus on expanding the brand and building a global coffee culture. By empowering his team to manage day-to-day operations, Schultz was able to concentrate on strategic growth, such as expanding Starbucks into new markets and developing the brand's identity.

Principle: Trust your team with operational tasks so you can focus on driving the vision and strategy of your business. Empowering others not only frees you to lead but also fosters a culture of accountability and ownership.

## 3. Innovate Continuously: Reed Hastings and Netflix

Lesson: Continuous innovation is essential for staying

relevant and competitive. Even when you're at the top, you must keep evolving to meet changing market demands.

Example: Reed Hastings, co-founder and CEO of Netflix, exemplified continuous innovation by transitioning the company from DVD rentals to streaming, and later, to original content production. Hastings understood that to stay ahead, Netflix had to constantly innovate and adapt to changing technologies and consumer preferences. This approach has allowed Netflix to dominate the entertainment industry and maintain its position as a leader in streaming services.

Principle: Never become complacent. Continuously seek ways to innovate, whether through new products, services, or business models. Staying ahead of the curve is key to long-term success.

## 4. Build a Legacy, Not Just a Business: Yvon Chouinard and Patagonia

Lesson: Building a business that makes a positive impact on the world creates a legacy that transcends profits. It's about contributing to society and the environment while achieving business success.

Example: Yvon Chouinard, founder of Patagonia, built his company around environmental sustainability and social responsibility. Patagonia's commitment to reducing its environmental footprint, supporting conservation efforts, and promoting sustainable practices has made it a model for how businesses can create value for all stakeholders, not just shareholders. Chouinard's legacy is one of a business that succeeds by doing good in the world.

Principle: Aspire to create a venture that not only generates financial success but also leaves an indelible mark on the world, positively influencing society and contributing to the well-being of the environment. Your legacy will be measured not only by your financial success but also by the contributions you make to the greater good.

## 5. Adapt to Change: Jeff Bezos and Amazon

Lesson: The ability to adapt to change is a critical component of business success. Markets, technologies, and consumer preferences are constantly evolving, and your business must be able to pivot when necessary.

Example: Jeff Bezos, the founder of Amazon, built his company with adaptability in mind. Amazon started as an online bookstore, but Bezos quickly recognized the potential for expansion into other product categories, eventually making Amazon "the everything store." Bezos also foresaw the importance of cloud computing, leading to the creation of Amazon Web Services (AWS), which has become a significant revenue stream for the company. Amazon's adaptability has allowed it to dominate multiple industries and continue growing in a rapidly changing market.

Principle: Cultivate a mindset of flexibility and openness to change, recognizing that the capacity to swiftly adapt to emerging opportunities and navigate unforeseen challenges is a fundamental prerequisite for sustaining growth and remaining relevant in an ever-evolving business landscape.

## 6. Focus on Long-Term Success: Warren Buffett and Berkshire Hathaway

Lesson: Patience and long-term thinking are vital for building a sustainable and successful business. Quick wins are tempting, but they shouldn't come at the expense of long-term goals.

Example: Warren Buffett, CEO of Berkshire Hathaway, is known for his long-term investment strategy. Buffett's approach is to invest in businesses with strong fundamentals and hold them for the long term, allowing value to grow over time. This focus on long-term success has made Berkshire Hathaway one of the most successful investment firms in the world and solidified Buffett's reputation as one of the greatest investors of all time.

Principle: Prioritize long-term goals over short-term

gains. Sustainable success comes from making decisions that will benefit your business in the years and decades to come.

## 7. Foster a Strong Company Culture: Tony Hsieh and Zappos

Lesson: A strong company culture is the foundation of a successful business. It influences employee satisfaction, customer loyalty, and overall business performance.

Example: Tony Hsieh, the late CEO of Zappos, was a pioneer in building a company culture centered on customer service, employee happiness, and core values. Hsieh believed that if you get the culture right, everything else – such as customer service and company performance – will fall into place. Zappos' unique culture became a key differentiator in the competitive online retail market, leading to its success and acquisition by Amazon.

Principle: Recognize the immense value of investing time and resources into cultivating and nurturing a robust company culture. A thriving, positive culture acts as a magnet for top talent, creates an environment that encourages innovation, and serves as the driving force behind enduring success.

## Final Thoughts: Your Journey Ahead

As you reflect on these lessons and principles, I encourage you to carry them forward on your entrepreneurial journey. Remember that being an entrepreneur is not just about managing a business – it's about leading with vision, inspiring others, and creating something that stands the test of time. Step confidently into your role as a visionary leader, entrusting your team with the responsibilities that will enable them to grow and excel. Cultivate a culture of continuous improvement, always seeking out new opportunities to innovate, evolve, and expand your business.

Your journey will be filled with challenges, but with the right mindset and strategies, you can overcome them and build a business that not only achieves financial success but also makes a meaningful impact on the world. Keep pushing forward, stay true to your vision, and never lose sight of the legacy you want to create.

The entrepreneurial journey is one of endless possibilities, and I wish you all the success and fulfillment as you continue to pursue your dreams. Your story is still being written, and the best is yet to come.

As we reach the end of this journey, it's essential to reflect on the core themes that have emerged throughout this book. We've explored the distinction between being an operator and becoming an entrepreneur, and the crucial role technology, automation, and scaling play in building a successful, sustainable business. Now, it's time to put these ideas into perspective and focus on the bigger picture: the mindset and strategy that drive entrepreneurial success.

## From Operator to Entrepreneur: A Mindset Shift

The evolution from operator to entrepreneur represents a pivotal shift in a business owner's trajectory, marking a profound transformation in both mindset and approach. It's not just about delegating tasks or automating processes – it's about fundamentally changing the way you think about your role and your business. As an operator, you're focused on the present: the daily tasks, the immediate problems that need solving. But as an entrepreneur, you're looking ahead, setting a vision for the future and guiding your company toward growth and innovation.

This shift in mindset is critical because it allows you to focus on what really matters: the long-term success of your business. By embracing technology, automating processes, and building a scalable business model, you create the freedom to step back from day-to-day operations and concentrate on strategy, leadership, and growth. You become the visionary that your business needs, and that's the key to unlocking its full potential. Here's a specific example demonstrating how technology adoption, automation, and a scalable model can allow a business owner to step back from daily tasks and focus on growth:

Emma founded FreshRoots, a specialty organic food supplier, with the mission of bringing high-quality, sustainably sourced ingredients to local restaurants and stores. Initially, she was deeply involved in every detail, from sourcing and inventory management to coordinating deliveries and handling customer inquiries. Her hands-on approach helped establish a loyal customer base, but as demand grew, Emma found herself constantly tied up in daily tasks, unable to focus on larger goals for the business.

To create a scalable model and free herself from day-to-day operations, Emma made three key investments:

1. Automating Inventory and Order Management: Emma implemented an inventory management system that integrated with her suppliers and customers, allowing for automated reordering and real-time tracking of stock levels. This system minimized stockouts and overstocking, reduced waste, and saved Emma hours each week that she previously spent managing inventory manually.
2. Customer Self-Service Portal: To enhance the customer experience and reduce repetitive tasks, Emma launched a self-service portal where clients could place orders, track deliveries, and manage invoices online. The portal allowed customers to quickly reorder items and view their order history, reducing the number of inquiries her team had to handle and increasing customer satisfaction.
3. Hiring Key Operational Roles and Delegating Responsibility: Emma hired an operations manager to oversee logistics and daily operations, empowering her team to make decisions based on clear guidelines. This delegation was essential in allowing Emma to move away from operational tasks and focus on the bigger picture.

Results: With technology, automation, and a strong operational team in place, Emma could step back from the daily grind and assume a strategic leadership role. Instead of spending her days resolving logistical issues, she began exploring new growth opportunities, such as expanding FreshRoots into e-commerce, building relationships with national distributors, and developing partnerships with other sustainable brands. She was able to work on branding, seek investment, and design a long-term vision for the company.

By embracing technology, automating processes, and building a scalable business model, Emma became the visionary her business needed. This shift allowed her to unlock FreshRoots' full potential, resulting in a 35 percent increase in revenue within two years, expanded distribution, and a clear path for future growth. Now, FreshRoots was no longer limited by Emma's time – it was built to grow independently, with Emma leading the way.

This example shows how focusing on scalable solutions allows a business owner to transition from operator to visionary, setting the stage for sustainable success and greater impact.

## The Power of Scaling: Why It Matters

Scaling is not just about growing your business; it's about growing smart. When you scale effectively, you increase efficiency, expand your market presence, and create a resilient company that can adapt to changes and seize new opportunities. Without scaling, even the most successful businesses can reach a plateau – unable to grow further because they're limited by their current capacity.

One entrepreneur who truly embodied the power of scaling is Lisa, the founder of a boutique marketing firm. Initially, Lisa handled every aspect of the business herself, from client acquisition to project delivery. She was successful, but she knew that without scaling, her growth would soon hit a ceiling. By implementing automation tools for client management and investing in a scalable team structure, Lisa was able to triple her client base within two years without burning out. She stepped back from the day-to-day tasks and focused on building strategic partnerships, growing her company's influence in the industry. Lisa's success wasn't just about working harder – it was about working smarter and thinking like an entrepreneur.

## The Entrepreneurial Roadmap: Your Next Steps

Now that you've learned the tools and strategies to evolve from an operator to an entrepreneur, it's time to apply them to your business. Here are some final actionable steps to take:

1. Adopt a Long-Term Vision: Think beyond the immediate challenges of running your business. Where do you want to be in five or ten years? Set clear, strategic goals and use them as a roadmap for your decisions.
2. Leverage Technology: Identify the technologies that can help streamline your operations and free up your time for strategic growth. Don't wait for your competitors to get ahead – start integrating these tools now.
3. Focus on Leadership: Build a team that shares your vision and can handle the day-to-day operations, allowing you to focus on what you do best: leading and innovating.
4. Commit to Scaling: Plan for growth by ensuring that your systems, processes, and team are scalable. This will give you the flexibility to expand without compromising quality or efficiency.

## Conclusion: A Final Word on Entrepreneurial Success

At the heart of every successful business is an entrepreneur who knows when to step back, strategize, and lead.

The entrepreneurial journey is not always easy, but it's incredibly rewarding. By adopting the right mindset, embracing technology, and focusing on scaling, you can create a business that not only thrives today but continues to grow and adapt in the future.

Remember, entrepreneurship is about more than just running a business – it's about building something that lasts. As you move forward, keep the principles in this book in mind and take the bold steps necessary to evolve as a leader and visionary. The path from operator to entrepreneur may be challenging, but it's the key to unlocking your business's full potential. Now, it's time to take action. The future of your business is in your hands – go build something extraordinary.

Here are reflection questions to help you apply the Financial Health and Profitability lessons to your business.

## Reflection Questions

### *Current Financial Assessment*

- How well do you understand your business's financial health? What key financial metrics do you regularly track?
- Are there areas where you feel financially vulnerable or over-leveraged?

### *Profitability Goals*

- What are your profitability goals for the next year? How do they compare to your current figures?
- What specific actions can you take to increase profitability without compromising quality?

### *Sustainable Financial Practices*

- What steps can you take to build a more financially resilient and sustainable business?
- How can you better allocate resources to support both growth and profitability?

# CHAPTER 11: CRAFTING A VISIONARY BUSINESS CULTURE

A company's culture is more than just a set of policies or an employee handbook – it's the embodiment of its values, beliefs, and the collective spirit that guides its actions and decisions. A visionary business culture serves as a compass, guiding employees toward a shared purpose while simultaneously creating a powerful competitive advantage that attracts customers, partners, and stakeholders alike. This chapter will guide you through creating a culture that aligns with your entrepreneurial vision, energizes your team, and drives sustainable growth.

## The Role of Culture in Visionary Leadership

A visionary business culture begins with clarity and purpose. As a leader, it's your role to set the vision, communicate it clearly, and model behaviors that exemplify it. Culture is the invisible hand that molds the workplace atmosphere, wielding significant influence over productivity, employee satisfaction, and the overall customer experience. By fostering a culture that aligns with your business goals and values, you create a foundation for long-term success.

Your culture becomes the lens through which everyone, from employees to customers, experiences your business. A robust, visionary culture:

- Builds trust and unity among team members.

- Inspires employees to go above and beyond.
- Creates a sense of belonging and loyalty.
- Attracts talent that aligns with your values and vision.

## Key Components of a Visionary Business Culture

### 1. Clear Core Values

Core values are the guiding principles that define what is acceptable and expected within your business. They serve as the moral compass for decision-making and employee behavior. When setting these values, consider what you want your company to be known for. Is it innovation, customer-centricity, integrity, or environmental responsibility? Choose values that resonate with both your mission and the everyday experiences of your team.

### 2. Strong Leadership and Consistency

Culture is built and reinforced through consistent leadership. Employees look to you for cues on behavior and priorities. Your actions set the standard, so lead by example. Demonstrate transparency, accountability, and a commitment to the culture you want to create. Over time, consistent leadership reinforces the values and principles that shape a cohesive and productive environment.

### 3. Inclusive and Open Communication

A visionary culture encourages open communication at all levels. When employees feel heard and valued, they become more engaged and committed. Promote transparency by sharing company updates, performance insights, and future plans. Encourage feedback and discussion, creating an environment where everyone feels empowered to contribute. This openness not only builds trust but also brings diverse ideas and innovation into your business.

## Promoting Transparency Through Regular Company Updates

1. Establish a Communication Schedule: Set a regular cadence for sharing updates with employees, such as weekly team meetings, monthly company newsletters, and quarterly all-hands meetings. Consistency builds trust and keeps employees informed about ongoing progress.
2. Share Performance Metrics and Key Insights: Present clear, relevant data on the company's performance. This can include metrics like revenue growth, customer satisfaction scores, project milestones, or cost savings. Use charts or dashboards to visualize this information, making it easy to understand. Regularly sharing performance insights keeps everyone aligned and motivated by the company's progress.
3. Discuss Future Plans and Strategic Goals: In addition to current performance, share updates on future initiatives, goals, and projects. Explain why these plans are important and how they align with the company's mission. Being open about future directions fosters a sense of purpose and helps employees see how their work contributes to long-term success.
4. Encourage Open Dialogue: After sharing updates, open the floor for questions, feedback, and suggestions. Use tools like anonymous Q&A, surveys, or live chats to make everyone comfortable participating. This approach promotes a culture of openness and ensures that employees feel heard.
5. Highlight Individual and Team Contributions: Recognize teams and individuals who have contributed to company success. This not only boosts morale but also reinforces the connection between personal effort and company goals.
6. Provide Access to Resources and Documentation: Make documents like quarterly reports, strategic plans, and project roadmaps available to employees

through shared platforms (e.g., a company intranet or digital workspace). This level of access builds trust and allows employees to engage with information at their own pace.

By promoting transparency through consistent communication, clear metrics, open dialogue, and resource access, you create a culture of trust and alignment. This approach empowers employees to contribute meaningfully and stay engaged with the company's mission and vision.

### 4. Emphasis on Growth and Development

A thriving culture supports personal and professional growth. Offer opportunities for your team to develop skills, take on new challenges, and advance their careers. This investment shows your employees that they are a valued part of the company's future. Consider providing mentorship, training programs, or resources for learning, especially in areas that align with your vision and goals. A culture that values growth and development will attract ambitious, forward-thinking individuals eager to contribute.

### 5. Recognition and Reward

Positive reinforcement is a powerful tool in shaping culture. Recognize and reward employees who exemplify your core values and contribute to the company's vision. Whether through formal recognition programs, bonuses, or informal appreciation, showing gratitude for hard work and dedication boosts morale and reinforces the behaviors that define your culture.

## Steps to Building Your Visionary Culture

### Step 1: Define Your Vision and Values

Take time to clarify your company's vision and core values. These should be more than statements on your website or a poster on the wall; they need to be actionable and lived every day. Involve your leadership team and, if possible, your employees in the process. Gather input on what's important, what works, and what doesn't. This will create a sense of ownership and ensure that your vision and values reflect the collective aspiration of your company.

## *Step 2: Create an Action Plan for Cultural Alignment*

Once you have a clear set of values, determine how they will be integrated into everyday operations. From onboarding new employees to performance evaluations, every process should reflect your culture. Consider establishing guidelines that show employees how to embody the values, from teamwork to problem-solving to customer interactions. Here's an example illustrating how a guideline can help employees embody the value of "Customer First."

Value: Customer First

Guideline: "Respond to all customer inquiries within 24 hours, providing clear, helpful information and offering solutions proactively."

How This Helps Employees Embody the Value:

This specific guideline reinforces the "Customer First" value by giving employees a concrete, actionable way to prioritize customer needs. Knowing they should respond within 24 hours sets a clear standard for responsiveness, ensuring customers feel valued and attended too quickly. Providing "clear, helpful information" reminds employees to communicate transparently and use language customers understand, building trust and satisfaction.

Additionally, the instruction to "offer solutions proactively" empowers employees to think beyond the basics and anticipate customer needs, creating a positive experience that aligns with the company's value of putting the customer first.

By following this guideline, employees consistently demonstrate "Customer First" behavior, fostering a customer-centric culture and enhancing overall satisfaction.

## *Step 3: Communicate and Reinforce the Vision*

Regular communication is essential in building and maintaining a visionary culture. Share stories that illustrate your values in action, highlight employee achievements, and celebrate milestones. Reinforce your vision through regular team meetings, company newsletters, and one-on-one check-ins. The more you communicate, the stronger your culture will become.

### Step 4: Model the Culture at Every Level

As the leader, you set the tone. Exhibit the behaviors you want to see in others. Encourage your managers to do the same, as consistency from all levels of leadership strengthens the culture. Ensure that your actions align with your values, especially when making tough decisions or handling challenges. This consistency builds trust and commitment to the vision across your team.

### Step 5: Measure, Evaluate, and Adapt

Culture is not static; it evolves with the business. Periodically assess your culture through employee feedback, surveys, and performance metrics. This feedback will reveal what's working, where improvements are needed, and how well your vision resonates with employees. Adapt as necessary, keeping your culture aligned with the needs and goals of the business. Remember, flexibility is key to a culture that grows with the company.

## Cultivating a Culture of Innovation and Adaptability

A visionary culture isn't just about maintaining the status quo; it's about fostering a mindset of growth and innovation. Encourage employees to think creatively, take calculated risks, and offer new ideas. By rewarding initiative and recognizing employees who contribute innovative solutions, you cultivate a team that is motivated to drive the business forward. This adaptability will serve your company well in a dynamic market environment, positioning it as a leader rather than a follower.

## Conclusion: Sustaining a Visionary Culture

Building a visionary culture takes time, commitment, and consistent effort. It's a journey that requires patience and dedication, but the rewards are substantial. When your team feels connected to a meaningful vision, they work with purpose and passion. A company with a vibrant, genuine culture becomes a magnet, attracting customers who value authenticity and forging deep bonds of loyalty, trust, and respect.

Building a visionary culture is a marathon, not a sprint. With unwavering clarity, deliberate intention, and steadfast consistency, you can cultivate an ecosystem where individuals flourish, innovation thrives, and everyone works together toward a shared purpose. This culture becomes the foundation for all future growth, sustaining your business as a place where employees, customers, and partners all feel connected to something greater than individual transactions.

## Reflection Questions

### *Current Culture Assessment*

- How would you describe your current business culture? What aspects reflect your vision, and where do you see gaps?
- Do your employees feel connected to the company's goals and values?

### *Building a Visionary Culture*

- What changes could you make to align your company culture more closely with your vision?
- How can you involve your team in creating and sustaining this culture?

### *Measuring Cultural Impact*

- How can you measure the effectiveness of your cultural initiatives?
- What actions can you take to keep your culture vibrant and meaningful as your business grows?

# CHAPTER 12:
# CREATING IMPACT BEYOND PROFIT

In the world of business, profitability is often the primary measure of success. However, in an increasingly conscious and interconnected world, companies that create a positive impact – both socially and environmentally – are thriving in new ways. Going beyond profit doesn't just benefit the world; it strengthens customer loyalty, enhances employee satisfaction, and builds a legacy that endures. This chapter will explore how you can make a meaningful impact with your business, aligning it with values that inspire both purpose and profit.

## The Case for Purpose-Driven Business

In today's marketplace, customers, investors, and employees are looking beyond numbers; they seek companies that stand for something. Purpose-driven businesses attract loyal customers who support their values, employees who find purpose in their work, and stakeholders who invest in sustainable futures. By fostering a culture that values purpose alongside profit, you set your business apart as a leader rather than just a player in the market.

The benefits of a purpose-driven business include:

- Customer Loyalty: Consumers are more likely to support businesses that align with their values, and 70 percent of consumers report preferring to buy from companies that demonstrate social responsibility.

- Employee Engagement: Purpose-oriented companies experience 40 percent higher employee retention, as employees are more motivated to work for organizations that make a difference.
- Brand Resilience: Businesses that go beyond profit build resilience, establishing a brand that people trust and want to see succeed.

## Defining Your Purpose

Your company's purpose should extend naturally from your vision, values, and goals. Consider the unique strengths, resources, and expertise you bring to the table. Your impact doesn't need to be on a global scale to be meaningful; it can start with small, local efforts or initiatives that directly benefit the communities where you operate.

To define your purpose, ask yourself:

- What issues or causes resonate most with you and your business?
- How can your business model support or address these issues?
- What skills, products, or resources do you have that could make a difference?

These questions will help you pinpoint your company's purpose and connect it to practical, actionable steps.

## Key Areas for Impact Beyond Profit

### 1. Environmental Sustainability

In the modern business landscape, sustainability has emerged as a crucial pillar, shaping the strategies and practices of forward-thinking organizations. By implementing eco-friendly practices, you demonstrate a commitment to reducing your environmental footprint. Whether through sustainable sourcing, reducing waste, or investing in renewable energy, environmental responsibility signals to customers that you care about the planet and its future.

## 2. Social Responsibility

Social impact can be achieved by supporting causes that align with your company's values. For example, you might focus on local community development, equal employment opportunities, or social justice issues. Companies that prioritize social impact are viewed as compassionate and community-minded, increasing goodwill and trust among consumers.

## 3. Ethical Practices

Creating impact beyond profit also means operating ethically in every area of business. From fair wages to transparent supply chains, ethical practices build trust and loyalty. When people know that they're supporting a company that treats its employees, suppliers, and customers fairly, they're more likely to stay loyal to your brand.

## 4. Employee Well-being and Development

A truly impactful business acknowledges that its employees are the lifeblood of the organization and invests in their well-being and growth accordingly. Supporting employee well-being through work-life balance, mental health resources, and career development initiatives creates a thriving workplace. When employees feel valued, they are more engaged, productive, and loyal, helping your business thrive while promoting individual growth.

## 5. Community Engagement

Involvement in your local community is a powerful way to make a positive impact. Whether through volunteer initiatives, partnerships with local organizations, or contributions to community projects, engaging with your community fosters goodwill and builds strong connections. Community support can take many forms, from sponsoring events to creating internships or apprenticeship programs.

# Implementing Purpose-Driven Strategies

### Align Purpose with Strategy

Integrate purpose into your business strategy to ensure it becomes a core part of your operations. Establish clear goals and benchmarks for how you will make an impact, whether through eco-friendly practices, social initiatives, or community involvement. Purpose isn't an afterthought – it's a foundational element that shapes every part of the business.

### Engage Your Employees

Involve employees in your purpose-driven initiatives. Whether through volunteer programs, environmental efforts, or diversity and inclusion initiatives, employee involvement ensures that your team feels personally invested in the company's mission. Employees who believe in a company's purpose are more motivated, engaged, and aligned with its goals.

### Communicate Impact

Share your purpose-driven efforts and achievements with customers, partners, and stakeholders. Transparency is key; let people know how you're making a difference, what challenges you face, and the progress you're making. Whether through social media, newsletters, or reports, communicating your impact encourages others to support your mission.

### Measure and Report Outcomes

To ensure that your efforts are impactful, establish metrics for tracking and evaluating progress. Whether you measure the amount of waste reduced, volunteer hours donated, or funds contributed, having tangible data shows that your commitment is real. Regularly review these metrics and be willing to adapt your approach to maximize positive impact.

### Building a Legacy of Impact

Creating impact beyond profit lays the foundation for a lasting legacy. Businesses that prioritize social responsibility, ethical practices, and sustainability gain respect and admiration from customers, employees, and the community. A purpose-driven legacy isn't just about what your business accomplishes during your tenure – it's about setting an example for future leaders and paving the way for lasting change.

A legacy of impact has lasting benefits:

- Inspires Future Leaders: Purpose-driven businesses set an example for future entrepreneurs, encouraging them to adopt similar principles.
- Enhances Brand Reputation: A commitment to impact builds trust and strengthens your brand's reputation, both locally and globally.
- Leaves a Positive Footprint: Making a difference within your community and industry contributes to a better world, creating a legacy that extends beyond financial success.

## Purpose as a Pathway to Profit and Fulfillment

Creating impact beyond profit transforms your business into more than just a financial entity; it becomes a force for positive change. By defining and acting on a clear purpose, you can inspire loyalty, encourage employee dedication, and build a resilient brand. As customers, employees, and investors increasingly seek purpose-driven businesses, you position your company as a leader in a conscious and connected world.

Incorporating purpose into your business model doesn't mean sacrificing profit; rather, it unlocks new avenues for growth, innovation, and loyalty. As you move forward, remember that every small action contributes to a greater impact. By staying true to your values and striving to make a positive difference, you create a business that is profitable, sustainable, and meaningful.

## Reflection Questions
### Defining Impact Goals
- What impact do you want your business to have beyond just financial success?
- How can you align your business practices with this vision of broader impact?

### Incorporating Purpose into Strategy
- How can you integrate social or environmental responsibility into your business model?
- Are there opportunities for partnerships or initiatives that align with your values?

### Tracking and Communicating Your Impact
- How will you measure and communicate the impact your business is making?
- What can you do to ensure your impact initiatives are sustainable and meaningful?

# CHAPTER 13:
# NURTURING THE ENTREPRENEUR WITHIN (BONUS CHAPTER)

*"Rest and self-care are so important. When you take time to replenish your spirit, it allows you to serve others from the overflow. You cannot serve from an empty vessel."*

– Eleanor Brown

This bonus chapter emphasizes the importance of self-care for entrepreneurs, providing practical advice on establishing morning and evening routines that promote health, happiness, and overall well-being. By prioritizing their physical, emotional, and mental health, entrepreneurs can ensure that they have the energy and clarity needed to lead their businesses effectively and enjoy the rewards of their hard work.

As an entrepreneur, you pour your heart and soul into your business. You work tirelessly to build something meaningful, to achieve your goals, and to leave a legacy. But amidst all the hustle and grind, it's easy to forget that the most important asset you have isn't your business, your network, or even your capital – it's you. Your physical, emotional, and mental well-being are the foundation upon which all your successes are built. Without them, everything else begins to crumble.

In this bonus chapter, I want to emphasize the importance of self-care and encourage you to adopt routines that nurture your health and happiness. By taking care of yourself, you not only enhance your ability to lead and grow your business, but you also ensure that you can enjoy the fruits of your labor for years to come.

## The Importance of Self-Care for Entrepreneurs

Running a business is demanding, and the pressures of entrepreneurship can take a toll on your health. Long hours, high stress, and the constant demands of leadership can lead to burnout if not managed properly. That's why it's crucial to prioritize self-care and make it a non-negotiable part of your daily routine.

Far from being an indulgence, self-care is an essential component of entrepreneurial success. Neglecting to prioritize your well-being can lead to burnout, impaired decision-making, and a diminished capacity to lead effectively, ultimately undermining the very business you have worked so hard to build. It's about maintaining the physical energy, emotional resilience, and mental clarity needed to navigate the challenges of entrepreneurship. When you're healthy and balanced, you're better equipped to make decisions, solve problems, and inspire your team. Moreover, self-care allows you to sustain your efforts over the long term, preventing burnout and ensuring that you can continue to lead your business effectively.

## Creating a Morning Routine for Success

Your morning routine sets the tone for the rest of the day. By starting your day with intentional practices that nurture your body and mind, you can boost your energy, focus, and productivity.

1. Wake Up Early: Waking up early gives you a head start on the day and allows you to begin your morning routine without feeling rushed. It's a time to focus on yourself before the demands of the business take over.
2. Hydrate and Nourish: Start your day by drinking a

glass of water to rehydrate your body after a night's sleep. Follow this with a nutritious breakfast that fuels your body with the energy it needs to perform at its best.
3. Exercise: Physical activity is a powerful way to boost your mood, increase your energy levels, and improve your overall health. Whether it's a morning jog, a yoga session, or a quick workout at the gym, make exercise a regular part of your morning routine.
4. Meditate or Practice Mindfulness: Taking a few minutes to meditate or practice mindfulness can help you clear your mind, reduce stress, and enhance your focus. This quiet time allows you to set your intentions for the day and approach your tasks with a calm, centered mindset.
5. Plan Your Day: Spend a few minutes reviewing your goals for the day. Prioritize your tasks and set clear objectives. Knowing what you need to accomplish will help you stay on track and make the most of your time.
6. Positive Affirmations: Start your day with positive affirmations that reinforce your goals and boost your confidence. Remind yourself of your strengths, your vision, and your ability to overcome challenges.

## Establishing an Evening Routine for Relaxation and Reflection

Just as a morning routine sets you up for a successful day, an evening routine helps you wind down, reflect, and prepare for the next day. It's a time to relax, recharge, and ensure that you get the rest you need.

1. Disconnect from Work: Set a specific time to stop working each evening. This boundary allows you to mentally and emotionally disconnect from the

business, reducing stress and promoting relaxation.
2. Reflect on Your Day: Take a few minutes to reflect on the day's achievements and challenges. What went well? What could have been done differently? Reflecting on your day helps you learn from your experiences and improves your decision-making.
3. Practice Gratitude: End your day on a positive note by practicing gratitude. Reflect on the things you're grateful for – whether it's personal achievements, relationships, or simple joys. Gratitude enhances your overall well-being and promotes a positive mindset.
4. Unwind with a Relaxing Activity: Engage in activities that help you relax and unwind. This could be reading a book, taking a warm bath, listening to music, or spending time with loved ones. Find what works best for you and make it a part of your evening routine.
5. Prepare for Tomorrow: Before bed, take a few minutes to plan for the next day. Review your schedule, set priorities, and make any necessary preparations. This helps you wake up feeling organized and ready to tackle the day.
6. Sleep Well: Prioritize sleep as a critical component of your health and well-being. Aim for seven to eight hours of quality sleep each night. Create a sleep-friendly environment by keeping your bedroom cool, dark, and quiet, and establish a consistent bedtime routine.

## The Entrepreneur's Most Important Asset: You

Remember, your business can only be as strong and resilient as you are. By taking care of yourself – physically, emotionally, and mentally – you're not just investing in your well-being; you're investing in the success of your business. Self-care is not a sign of weakness; it's a demonstration of strength and wisdom.

## FROM OPERATOR TO ENTREPRENEUR

As you continue your entrepreneurial journey, I encourage you to make self-care a priority. By creating and maintaining healthy routines, you'll be better equipped to lead your business, make sound decisions, and navigate the challenges that come your way. More importantly, you'll ensure that you can enjoy the fruits of your labor – a healthy, happy life surrounded by the people and achievements that matter most.

I wish you a balanced and fulfilling journey as an entrepreneur. May you achieve not only the success you envision for your business but also the well-being and happiness that make the journey truly worthwhile. Take care of yourself, nurture your dreams, and continue to lead with vision and purpose.

This bonus chapter emphasizes the critical role that self-care plays in the life of an entrepreneur. It provides practical advice on establishing morning and evening routines that promote health, happiness, and overall well-being. By prioritizing physical, emotional, and mental health, entrepreneurs can ensure they have the energy, clarity, and resilience needed to lead their businesses effectively and enjoy the rewards of their hard work.

Below are some examples of famous entrepreneurs who have made significant lifestyle choices that emphasize the importance of self-care, along with reflections on the meaning of significance and contribution in their lives.

## 1. Arianna Huffington – Prioritizing Sleep and Well-Being

Background: Arianna Huffington, co-founder of The Huffington Post and founder of Thrive Global, is a strong advocate for the importance of sleep and well-being. After collapsing from exhaustion in 2007, Huffington realized the impact that lack of sleep and burnout was having on her health and success.

Lifestyle Choices: Huffington made significant changes to her lifestyle, prioritizing sleep, meditation, and relaxation.

She has since become a vocal advocate for the importance of rest, writing books like The Sleep Revolution and launching Thrive Global, a company focused on improving well-being and performance through better health practices.

Meaning of Significance and Contribution: For Huffington, significance and contribution come from helping others achieve balance and well-being in their lives. Through her work at Thrive Global, she has contributed to a cultural shift that recognizes the importance of self-care in achieving success. Her message is clear: entrepreneurs can only reach their full potential when they take care of their health and prioritize rest.

## 2. Richard Branson – Maintaining Work-Life Balance and Physical Fitness

Background: Richard Branson, the founder of the Virgin Group, is known not only for his entrepreneurial success but also for his adventurous spirit and commitment to maintaining a healthy work-life balance. Branson believes that taking care of one's physical health is essential to sustaining the energy needed for business leadership.

Lifestyle Choices: Branson starts his day with exercise, whether it's kite surfing, playing tennis, or cycling. He believes that physical activity is key to staying sharp and energized. Branson also emphasizes the importance of family time and maintaining a balance between work and personal life.

Meaning of Significance and Contribution: For Branson, significance is about living life to the fullest and using his influence to make a positive impact on the world. His philanthropic efforts, such as the Virgin Unite foundation, reflect his commitment to contributing to society and supporting causes that matter to him. Branson's lifestyle choices show that success is not just about business achievements but also about personal fulfillment and giving back.

## 3. Oprah Winfrey – Mindfulness, Meditation, and

## Personal Growth

Background: Oprah Winfrey, media mogul and philanthropist, has long been an advocate for mindfulness, meditation, and personal growth. Winfrey credits much of her success to her commitment to self-care and spiritual well-being.

Lifestyle Choices: Winfrey practices meditation daily and incorporates mindfulness into her routine. She also focuses on gratitude and self-reflection as part of her personal growth journey. Winfrey's morning routine includes exercise, reading, and journaling, which she believes are essential for maintaining mental clarity and emotional balance.

Meaning of Significance and Contribution: Winfrey's significance comes from her ability to inspire and empower others through her work. Her contributions to society are vast, from her philanthropic initiatives, such as the Oprah Winfrey Leadership Academy for Girls in South Africa, to her efforts in promoting education, literacy, and well-being. Winfrey's commitment to self-care allows her to continue making meaningful contributions to the lives of millions around the world.

## 4. Jack Dorsey – Routine, Discipline, and Mental Clarity

Background: Jack Dorsey, co-founder of Twitter and Square, is known for his disciplined approach to daily routines. Dorsey emphasizes the importance of structure and consistency in maintaining mental clarity and productivity.

Lifestyle Choices: Dorsey follows a strict daily routine that includes waking up at 5:00 a.m., meditating for an hour, and then exercising. He also practices intermittent fasting and adheres to a minimalist lifestyle, believing that simplicity and discipline help him stay focused and creative. Dorsey's evening routine involves reflection and winding down without digital distractions.

Meaning of Significance and Contribution: Dorsey's

significance lies in his ability to innovate and create platforms that have transformed the way people communicate and conduct business. His contributions extend beyond his companies, as he is also involved in philanthropic efforts, including donations to social justice causes and education initiatives. Dorsey's disciplined lifestyle enables him to maintain the focus and mental clarity needed to lead his business and make a positive impact.

## 5. Bill Gates – Lifelong Learning and Philanthropy

Background: Bill Gates, co-founder of Microsoft, is not only known for his contributions to technology but also for his commitment to lifelong learning and philanthropy. Gates is an avid reader and believes that continuous learning is key to personal and professional growth.

Lifestyle Choices: Gates dedicates time each day to reading and learning about a wide range of topics. He also emphasizes the importance of curiosity and staying informed about global issues. Gates practices self-care by ensuring he maintains a balanced lifestyle, which includes time for reflection, exercise, and family.

Meaning of Significance and Contribution: For Gates, significance is deeply tied to his philanthropic work through the Bill and Melinda Gates Foundation. His contributions to global health, education, and poverty alleviation are driven by his belief that everyone deserves the opportunity to live a healthy and productive life. Gates' commitment to lifelong learning and his focus on making a positive impact are central to his legacy.

## 6. Jeff Bezos – Prioritizing Sleep and Work-Life Balance

Background: Jeff Bezos, the founder of Amazon, is one of the richest individuals in the world. Despite the intense demands of building and running a global empire, Bezos emphasizes the importance of sleep and work-life balance.

Lifestyle Choices: Bezos is known for prioritizing eight

hours of sleep each night, which he believes is crucial for making high-quality decisions. He also emphasizes the importance of not rushing through his morning routine, preferring to have a relaxed start to the day with time for breakfast with his family. Bezos schedules his most important meetings for the morning when he feels most alert and avoids overloading his schedule with meetings later in the day.

Significance and Contribution: Bezos' approach to work-life balance has allowed him to maintain a high level of productivity and creativity, which has been key to Amazon's success. His focus on creating value for customers and long-term vision has had a profound impact on global commerce and technology. Bezos' balanced lifestyle enables him to sustain the energy and mental clarity needed to drive Amazon's growth and innovation.

### 7. Elon Musk – Balancing Intense Work Schedules with Personal Wellness

Background: Elon Musk, the CEO of Tesla and SpaceX, is known for his intense work ethic and ambitious goals, such as making humanity a multiplanetary species. Musk's work schedule is famously demanding, but he also recognizes the importance of personal wellness.

Lifestyle Choices: Musk has admitted to working long hours, often exceeding eighty to a hundred hours per week. However, he has also made efforts to ensure that he gets sufficient sleep, usually aiming for about six hours per night. Musk values efficiency and maximizes his productivity by scheduling his day in five-minute blocks. Despite his intense work schedule, he prioritizes spending time with his children and engaging in activities that help him relax and recharge, such as watching movies and reading science fiction.

Significance and Contribution: Musk's relentless drive and willingness to push the boundaries of technology have led to significant advancements in electric vehicles, space exploration, and renewable energy. His lifestyle reflects the balance between intense focus on work and the need for personal time, allowing him to achieve his visionary goals while maintaining his well-being.

## 8. Sheryl Sandberg – Advocating for Work-Life Integration

Background: Sheryl Sandberg, the COO of Facebook and author of Lean In, is a prominent advocate for work-life integration, particularly for women in the workplace. Sandberg has openly discussed the challenges of balancing a demanding career with personal life.

Lifestyle Choices: Sandberg emphasizes the importance of setting boundaries to achieve work-life balance. She is known for leaving the office at 5:30 p.m. every day to have dinner with her children, a practice she maintains even with her busy schedule. Sandberg also prioritizes exercise and mindfulness, recognizing that taking care of her physical and mental health is essential for her effectiveness as a leader.

Significance and Contribution: Sandberg's advocacy for work-life integration has inspired many professionals to seek balance in their lives while pursuing ambitious careers. Her contributions to discussions on gender equality, leadership, and work-life balance have had a significant impact on corporate culture and the lives of working women around the world.

## 9. Warren Buffett – The Importance of Routine and Simplicity

Background: Warren Buffett, CEO of Berkshire Hathaway, is known for his simple lifestyle and adherence to routine, despite being one of the wealthiest individuals in the world. Buffett's approach to life and business is characterized by a focus on simplicity and long-term thinking.

Lifestyle Choices: Buffett maintains a highly consistent daily routine, which includes reading extensively, playing bridge, and enjoying simple pleasures like drinking Coca-

Cola. He is also known for his modest living, continuing to reside in the same house he bought in 1958. Buffett's lifestyle reflects his belief in the importance of maintaining mental clarity and focus through simplicity and routine.

Significance and Contribution: Buffett's approach to life and investing has made him one of the most successful investors of all time. His commitment to simplicity and long-term thinking has not only benefited his life but has also provided valuable lessons to countless others in the fields of finance and business. Buffett's contributions to philanthropy through the Giving Pledge further highlight his belief in the importance of significance and contribution.

## 10. Mark Zuckerberg – Maintaining Focus Through Minimalism

Background: Mark Zuckerberg, co-founder and CEO of Facebook, is known for his minimalist lifestyle, which helps him maintain focus on his work. Zuckerberg's simplicity in both his personal life and leadership style reflects his commitment to efficiency and clarity.

Lifestyle Choices: Zuckerberg famously wears the same style of clothing every day – a gray t-shirt and jeans – believing that reducing the number of decisions he must make each day allows him to focus on more important tasks. He also follows a structured daily routine, which includes exercise, spending time with his family, and working on his long-term goals for Facebook.

Significance and Contribution: Zuckerberg's minimalist approach to life has enabled him to stay focused on building and expanding Facebook, which has become one of the most influential companies in the world. His emphasis on social connectivity and innovation has contributed to significant changes in how people communicate and interact online. Zuckerberg's leadership style and lifestyle choices underscore the importance of focus, simplicity, and long-term vision in achieving success.

## 11. Tony Robbins – Prioritizing Physical and Mental Health

Background: Tony Robbins, a renowned life coach, author, and entrepreneur, emphasizes the importance of physical and mental health as key components of success. Robbins' work focuses on personal development, peak performance, and helping others achieve their goals.

Lifestyle Choices: Robbins is known for his rigorous self-care routine, which includes daily meditation, cold plunges, and a commitment to physical fitness. He also practices gratitude and visualization, which he believes are essential for maintaining a positive mindset and achieving his goals. Robbins emphasizes the importance of energy management, ensuring that he is always in peak physical and mental condition to serve his clients and audiences.

Significance and Contribution: Robbins' focus on health and wellness has been a cornerstone of his success as a coach and entrepreneur. His teachings on personal development and peak performance have helped millions of people around the world achieve greater success and fulfillment. Robbins' lifestyle choices highlight the importance of taking care of oneself to effectively lead and inspire others.

## 12. Jack Ma – Balancing Work with Meditation and Tai Chi

Background: Jack Ma, the co-founder of Alibaba Group, is one of China's most prominent entrepreneurs. Known for his unconventional leadership style and philosophy, Ma emphasizes the importance of balance, mental health, and personal well-being.

Lifestyle Choices: Ma practices Tai Chi, a traditional Chinese martial art, as part of his daily routine. He believes that Tai Chi helps him maintain mental clarity, reduce stress, and stay grounded. Ma also incorporates meditation into his routine, which he credits with helping him stay focused and make better decisions. He emphasizes the importance of balancing work with personal time and encourages his employees to find balance in their lives as well.

Significance and Contribution: Ma's commitment to balance and well-being has been integral to his success as a leader and entrepreneur. His contributions to e-commerce and technology have had a profound impact on the global economy, particularly in China. Ma's lifestyle choices reflect his belief in the importance of maintaining mental and physical health to achieve long-term success.

## 13. Mark Cuban – The Importance of Exercise and Mental Stimulation

Background: Mark Cuban, billionaire entrepreneur and owner of the Dallas Mavericks, is known for his proactive approach to fitness and mental stimulation. Cuban's diverse career, which spans technology, media, and sports, is driven by his commitment to staying physically and mentally fit.

Lifestyle Choices: Cuban emphasizes the importance of regular exercise, which he believes is crucial for maintaining energy and focus. He works out for at least an hour every day, mixing activities like basketball, running, and weightlifting. Cuban is also a voracious reader, dedicating time each day to reading and learning about a wide range of topics, which keeps him informed and mentally sharp.

Significance and Contribution: Cuban's emphasis on physical fitness and continuous learning has been instrumental in his success as an entrepreneur and investor. His contributions to the business world, particularly in technology and sports, are driven by his ability to stay ahead of trends and make informed decisions. Cuban's lifestyle underscores the importance of exercise and mental stimulation in maintaining peak performance.

## Final Thoughts: Embracing Self-Care and Contribution

The lifestyles of these successful entrepreneurs demonstrate that self-care is not a luxury but a necessity for sustained success and impact. By prioritizing physical, mental, and emotional well-being, these leaders have been able to achieve remarkable success while also making significant contributions to society.

As you continue your entrepreneurial journey, consider how you can incorporate self-care practices into your daily routine. Whether it's through maintaining a consistent sleep schedule like Jeff Bezos, embracing simplicity like Warren Buffett, or committing to physical fitness like Tony Robbins, taking care of yourself is essential for maintaining the energy, focus, and resilience needed to lead your business and make a lasting impact.

Recognize that genuine success transcends mere financial accomplishments; it is equally defined by the profound impact of your contributions to the lives of others and the enduring legacy you create. By focusing on making a positive difference in the world and leaving a lasting mark on your industry and community, you can achieve a deeper sense of fulfillment and purpose that goes beyond material wealth. By prioritizing self-care and living with purpose, you can create a life and business that are not only successful but also meaningful and fulfilling.

Entrepreneurship is not just about building a business – it's about nurturing the spirit of innovation, leadership, and resilience within yourself. As you embark on the journey from operator to entrepreneur, it's important to remember that personal growth plays a key role in professional success. This journey is as much about self-discovery as it is about developing the right business strategies.

Throughout this book, we've explored the essential steps to grow your business, from embracing technology to scaling for success. But to truly thrive as an entrepreneur, you need to nurture your inner well-being, stay aligned with your purpose, and maintain a balanced mindset. After all, the most successful entrepreneurs are those who lead with clarity, focus, and a sense of purpose.

As a certified Chopra wellness teacher, I've seen

firsthand how crucial it is for entrepreneurs to cultivate both mental and physical wellness alongside their business pursuits. Wellness is not just a personal goal – it directly impacts your ability to lead effectively, manage stress, and make sound decisions. By integrating wellness practices into your daily routine, you can foster a mindset that promotes growth, resilience, and creativity.

This chapter is dedicated to helping you nurture the entrepreneur within by offering strategies to maintain balance and wellness on your entrepreneurial journey. Whether through mindfulness, meditation, or wellness practices, prioritizing your personal well-being will enhance your ability to lead with purpose and vision.

Here are reflection questions to help you apply the Wellness and Balance as a Leader lessons to your business.

## Reflection Questions

### *Personal Well-Being Check*

- How would you rate your current work-life balance on a scale of 1 to 10?
- What areas of your life could benefit from more balance or wellness-focused practices?

### *Integrating Wellness into Leadership*

- How can you set an example of well-being and balance for your team?
- Are there wellness practices you could incorporate into your daily or weekly routine to support your role?

### *Sustaining Long-Term Energy and Focus*

- What practices or routines help you stay energized and focused?
- How can you ensure that you're investing in your well-being to avoid burnout?

## Extending Our Journey Together

As you continue your journey, I invite you to connect with me for one-on-one consultations. Whether you're looking to explore wellness practices to support your entrepreneurial journey or seeking business advice on how to implement the strategies outlined in this book, I'm here to help. My experience as both an entrepreneur and a wellness teacher uniquely position me to guide others in achieving both business success and personal fulfillment.

Feel free to reach out if you're interested in personalized guidance or deeper insights into balancing entrepreneurship with wellness. Together, we can ensure that you not only build a thriving business but also nurture the best version of yourself along the way.

www.ingramcontent.com/pod-product-compliance
Lightning Source LLC
Chambersburg PA
CBHW052152220526
45471CB00004B/1637